THE
CAGED IN
HEART

The
Caged In
Heart

How Your Childhood Wounds
are Affecting Your Adult Life

Trillion Small, MS

Clovercroft Publishing

The Caged In Heart:
How Your Childhood Wounds are Affecting Your Adult Life

©2015 by Trillion Small

Published by Clovercroft Publishing, Franklin, Tennessee

Scripture is used from the New King James Version, © 1982 by
Thomas Nelson, Inc. All rights reserved. Used by permission.

The names, details, and circumstances may have been changed to
protect the privacy of those mentioned in this publication.

This publication is not intended as a substitute
for the advice of health care professionals.

Cover and Interior Design by Suzanne Lawing

Editing by Gail Fallen

Printed in the United States of America

978-1-942587-32-3

I DEDICATE THIS BOOK TO THE FOLLOWING:

To God, first and foremost, because everything that I do is because of Him and for His glory.

To Lauren Capozzi, my former counseling supervisor at The Refuge Center for Counseling in Franklin, Tennessee. Thank you for being a secure base where I could learn to take off my mask and be vulnerable.

To Amy Alexander and The Refuge Center family. Thank you for creating a warm and loving atmosphere that created space for me to just "BE" and grow into the woman that I am today.

To Dr. Susan Lahey, one of my former doctoral professors at Trevecca Nazarene University. Thank you for caring so much about me and seeing right through to my pain even though I was silent. Thank you for teaching me that our tears can be gifts to others.

Scriptural Foundation for The Caged in Heart

Isaiah 61:1-4 (NIV)
"He has sent me to bind up the brokenhearted, to proclaim freedom for the captives and release from darkness for the prisoners . . . to comfort all who mourn . . . to bestow on them a crown of beauty instead of ashes . . . They will rebuild the ancient ruins and restore the places long devastated; they will renew the ruined cities that have been devastated for generations."

CONTENTS

FOREWORD

There are books I've read that I believe are essential and necessary for our journey of development. This is one of them. Trillion Small has courageously tackled a tough issue and provided us all immeasurable insight. As a faith leader, I've often met with hypervigilant people who struggled in the area of discernment. The bridge between the two is often long, but Trillion shortens the distance by providing practical and profound principles.

It is a fact that God's hopes for His people are chronicled in Isaiah 61, yet many are unable to realize it because of the un-reconciled issues in our lives. You cannot fix what you are not willing to face. This book challenges us to confront deep wounds in our past and chart a course for healing and wholeness. When we are whole, our relationships get better and ultimately our communities. If we don't deal with the critical issue of hypervigilance, we run the risk of pushing away those whom God sends in our lives to help us.

Discernment is the key. I believe every barrier to spiritual discernment must be knocked down. This book begins that process one brick at a time. It is not for the faint at heart. This book is for those who refuse to be defined by their past and are willing to embrace a new future free from assumptions and erroneous perceptions about everything and everybody. If you are willing to take this journey, do so with great expectancy. You will not be disappointed. This is a masterpiece.

—BISHOP JOSEPH WARREN WALKER III, *Senior Pastor, Mt. Zion Baptist Church, Nashville, Tennessee; Presiding Bishop, Full Gospel Baptist Church Fellowship International*

PREFACE

Many children grow into adulthood with unresolved childhood attachment injuries (internal wounds) that often originated in the home and affected his or her view of self. It doesn't matter if the wound was intentional or not, it still can have the same adverse effects on the child and his or her intimate relationships later in life. One effect is *relational hypervigilance*. Relational hypervigilance can produce issues in your mental, emotional, physical, and spiritual functioning. It makes living alone difficult and hinders your ability to form strong, healthy, and secure relationships.

Consequently, the purpose of this book is twofold. First, the first four chapters of this book are designed to shine light on the internal wounds that often go unnoticed and to provide a means of relief from the overwhelming burdens they have caused you in relationships. The goal of these chapters is to increase your awareness to the many facets of abuse and how to break the cycle.

Second, the last three chapters of this book are designed to look more specifically at one effect of abuse, and that is relational hypervigilance. I will provide insight and guidance on how to rest your overworked hyperactive threat system. This system is the internal system in your brain that alerts you when real or perceived danger is near (i.e., the limbic system). If you are hypervigilant, your alarm is always going off, and this is exhausting for you. In this book you will gain a better understanding of abuse and its cycle, how to break the cycle, and how to find beauty in the ashes of your past experiences.

❤

How I define "childhood attachment injuries" in the book: The word abuse is characterized by an experience that was physical, sexual, mental, or emotional that impacted one's view of self at the core. This book specifically will focus on the attachment injuries that happened as a child/teen. These are injuries that leave no physical evidence, because they are internal. These are "heart" injuries that leave you feeling negative about yourself and others. This includes witnessing physical and/or psychological domestic violence (i.e., seeing parents hit one another, name-call, or yell) or having over-protective parents, rejecting/non-supportive parents, present but emotionally absent parents, parents who ignore or withdraw from you, etc.) *The words trauma, abuse, childhood attachment injuries, and internal wounds will all be used interchangeably in the context of this book.*

How I define "relational hypervigilance" in the book: A relationally hypervigilant individual is one who is often on the alert for real (or perceived) threats in an intimate relationship. This includes threats of rejection, abandonment, neglect, and abuse. They will do all they can to prevent anything bad from happening, even if it means clinging or running before it happens. They are often anxious about another's behaviors, thoughts, feelings, etc., and struggle with ambiguity because they "manage" life by being in control. This person often has to "steal" trust in order to trust (i.e., phone searching, social-media snooping, requesting passwords, etc.).

Essentially, a relationally hypervigilant person is very low in their ability to trust others and, at times, can have a negative view of self. An insecure attachment with both the self and others is oftentimes the result. The paradox is that this person can push safe people away and cling to unsafe people.

How I define "relational discernment" in the book: Relational discernment is the ability to perceive people without having foreknowledge of them. You can discern both positive and negative things (good and evil).

This book is for individuals in a clinical and/ or spiritual work setting (i.e., psychologists, therapists, social workers, the clergy, etc. . . .) as well as for anyone who has attachment wounds, interacts with those wounded, or simply desires to gain a basic working knowledge of abuse and how someone can take such a horrible experience and find a ray of hope from it. Most importantly, this book is for individuals who are struggling with relational hypervigilance and are physically, mentally, emotionally, and spiritually exhausted from always being on the alert for threats that oftentimes are non-existent. Although this book's focus is on intimate relationships, the material can be applied to other relationships as well.

❤

This book is not designed to provide you with all there is to know about trauma. Instead, it is written to shift a maladaptive life-consuming symptom (hyper-vigilance) into one that is adaptive and can be used to bring about freedom, restoration, and a new life to the internal and relational world of those who have been wounded.

CHAPTER ONE

TRAUMA AND ITS EFFECTS

AS AN ADULT I have very few recollections of my childhood. This began to bother me because I realized that there was more to my "childhood amnesia" than me just forgetting. As I dug and dug more, I developed a better understanding of dissociation.[1] There are various ways a person can dissociate. The way I typically did was by emotionally and physically diverting my attention from what was painful so that I didn't have to acknowledge what was going on. Two specific ways I did this was by taking myself to another place through reading and sleeping. You may be asking, "Well, if you don't remember your childhood, how do you know what you did to dissociate?" Great question. I know what I did because I also did it as an adult (and I still have to be mindful at times not to when I am emotionally overwhelmed). Some people turn to food, alcohol, drugs, sex, television, and a multitude of other things to numb, but I chose reading (or education) and sleeping.

I was eager to heal from my past, so my therapist

and I began Eye Movement Desensitization Reprocessing (EMDR) treatment.[2] Toward the end of one of our processing sessions I had the thought, *I don't have to go to sleep anymore.* That was a light-bulb moment for me, because up to that point, I never realized that sleep was what I did when I was emotionally exhausted. After that day, I was able to reflect on all the times I used sleep to free myself from what I was feeling. I even had a dream that following night and God confirmed that I used dissociation to escape what was painful. Here is the dream:

> *I was in a room alone while two other girls were in the room next door talking about this man's daughter. The man overheard them saying mean things, so he stormed into their room and grabbed them both by the arm. Meanwhile, I am still in the other room next door by myself. I immediately get scared and angry, but I do nothing about it because I feel powerless. Instead, I float to the top of the ceiling and try my best to make myself shrink really small so he couldn't see me if he came in the room. It wasn't working, so I just wrapped myself in a blanket and placed my head in my folded arms so that I didn't have to look. I stayed as still as possible hoping that he wouldn't see or hear me and get mad at me too. After he left I floated back down to the ground and walked out to talk to some of the other girls. My comment to them was, "I'm just not trying to get on his bad side." With that, I walked off.*

Although this was a dream, it is exactly what I did.

If I felt powerless over something, I would just turn away and let the storm pass. As an adult I have more control over what I submit myself to, so instead of always turning away, at times I would find myself *running away* instead. I used to call myself a *runner,* because at the slightest inclination of rejection or intense uncomfortable emotions, I would take off and/ or cut off the friendship/relationship.

Not only would I do this with people, but I also subconsciously did this with God. It took a person looking me in the eyes and sharing a prophecy from God with me before I was able to realize this. The man looked at me and said, "Trillion, God says that He is pursuing you. He needs you to stop, turn around, and let Him catch you." I actually wasn't comforted by this word; I felt frustrated because I had no idea how I was "running" from Him. I thought I was doing everything He wanted me to. I soon realized that I wasn't necessarily running away from Him, but I was running away from my past, trying to distance myself as much as possible. But He wanted me to stop running and face whatever I was afraid of—not by myself, but with Him. As I began to slow my pace, God was able to reveal to me that I was dealing with symptoms similar to Post Traumatic Stress Disorder (PTSD[3] or Developmental Trauma,[4] which is not a formal diagnosis yet). The two most prevalent symptoms that I experienced were dissociation and hypervigilance. Our primary focus will be the latter.

HOW DOES IT AFFECT US?

Trauma can change the trajectory of a person's life forever if help is not sought out. It can increase the likelihood of emotional symptoms such as shame, sadness, depression, and anxiety. It also can increase one's susceptibility to psychological and physical symptoms such as poor concentration, catastrophizing, insomnia, tension, irritation, and various other medical conditions, including irritable bowel syndrome, migraines, and fibromyalgia. Along with these things, a person who has experienced trauma may have more academic, legal, and social problems than a person who has not or has healed from their experiences.

Over the years, I have discovered that trauma is a subjective experience. What may be traumatic for some may not be for others. I do believe that there are other factors in play when it comes to this, such as levels of social support, emotional intelligence, and the capacity to regulate emotions. However, what you experience as traumatic *is* traumatic. Minimizing your experience only prolongs the suffering. I began to realize this when working with adults who experienced childhood trauma. Many incidents seemed very minor in retrospect, but to their child self, it was traumatic.

Trauma can be overt and covert. Overt trauma would be a direct attack, such as physical and sexual abuse. Covert trauma is more subtle, such as being ignored, controlled, or manipulated by a loved one. Either way, both send a message of worthlessness to the receiver. Sometimes it is not what WAS done to us that hurt the most. It is what WAS NOT done to us that hurts the most. I have seen women who have been molested express the greatest anger and sadness as they talk about how they were NOT protected. Yes, the event hurt them as well, but the deeper wound came from realizing that nobody was there to protect them! What about you? What was done to you or wasn't done for you that has left a scar on your heart?

One of my traumatic incidents happened when I was in the fourth or fifth grade. I remember sitting outside on the curb after school, waiting on my mom to pick me up, and a little boy sat next to me and kicked my foot. He said that my legs were fat because they jiggled. In my adult rational mind, I didn't think it was a big deal, but to that nine- or ten-year-old little girl, it cut deep. I found myself—even as an adult—wanting to wear things that covered up my legs because I didn't think they looked "good enough." All because of what a ten-year-old little boy said to me.

IS YOUR PAST PRESENT?

The thought may be crossing your mind that my situation was NOT traumatic. However, it became traumatic when my past was present and affected the way that I lived and adjusted my life around what happened. It reminds me of a client who was self-conscious while eating out because, as a child, her dad made her feel fat. She figured if her dad thought she looked fat, then surely strangers would too.

Are you aware of past situations that still have an

active role in your present life? What do you do or don't do because of something that happened to you years ago? Maybe you don't strive for excellence because you were once told you weren't good enough. Maybe you shy away from men because your daddy never told you that you were beautiful. Maybe you are angry with God because your earthly dad was mean to you. Maybe you bundle all of your emotions inside and compartmentalize them because someone once told you to suck it up. Maybe you strive for perfection in order to earn approval from that person that once rejected you.

Our behaviors, habits, temperament, and triggers all begin to make sense when we understand how our past is active in our lives today. The more self-aware we are, the closer we get to a place of healing and restoration from those things that afflict us. Trauma tends to put tented lens over our eyes so that life after the trauma begins to look and feel just like the trauma experience. So, for example, if you were ignored often as a child then, as an adult, you may find yourself immediately increasingly anxious when somebody doesn't respond to your text, call, or email. If that is the case, then being ignored (or feeling like you are being ignored) is a trigger point for you.

All of our experiences teach us something about ourselves and others. One experience may teach you that people are trustworthy, and another may teach you that you aren't loved. A parent showing up to his or her child's games most likely will instill positive thoughts in the child that they matter, they are important, and they are supported. On the other hand, a parent not showing up to the child's games may instill negative thoughts in the child, such as "I'm not good enough," "It's my fault," "I'm rejected," "I'm a disappointment," and "I'm all alone."

We carry both the negative and positive thoughts on into adulthood with us, and they help us determine how to respond to life's situations. I had an adult client whose parents got mad at him every time he did something wrong, even if he was just being a kid. Their look of disgust was wedged into his brain so deeply that when they or anyone else in his adult life looked at him like that, he would think, *I'm a big disappointment.* This negative thought handicapped him, so to speak, by keeping him in the "safe" zone, not ruffling any feathers or doing anything that may cause others to see him as a disappointment. This became his normal way of living until he realized he could develop a new "healthy normal" for his life.

INTERNAL AND EXTERNAL CONFLICTS

When our past is present, it produces both internal and external conflicts. It is often said that we can be our worst critics. I've also heard the saying "the enemy is inner me." I call it inner self-harassment and inner self-brutality. You can find this war going on in your mind. If we were to make a motion picture of your thoughts, it probably would be full of three-year-old "fear clips" that are displayed through tantrums; followed by fifteen-year-old sassy, rebellious clips; followed by twenty-, thirty-, forty-, and fifty- year-old lost, lonely, angry, and confused clips. I believe Internal Family Systems (IFS[5]), a therapy model, works wonders to really capture what each part of us needs and fears. Here is an example of the internal and external worlds colliding in conflict:

The Case of Anne
(*Not a Real Client*)

Anne is a twenty-nine-year-old female. Her presenting issues were depression, anxiety, and low self-esteem. After mapping out her different internal family parts through IFS, she discovered she had three different parts that were active in her life. She had a child part that was scared and lonely; a teenage part that was very anxious, controlling, and rejecting; and an older part that was angry, bitter, lost, and also lonely. Her trigger points, which were rooted in her childhood, were (1) feeling like others were using her, (2) feeling like others were rejecting her, and (3) feeling like she didn't fit in. When these trigger points were activated (from real or perceived threats), her child part would come out for a brief moment, afraid and lonely, but before she would allow herself to be overtaken by the sadness, her teenage part would emerge, rejecting the person before they could reject her. In order to protect her child part, Anne's teenage part would take over, going into isolation mode for protection. While in isolation, her adult part would come out, angry that she was being treated that way, bitter that she didn't have anyone to protect her, and incensed that she is lonely (again), which is the very thing she tried to avoid in the beginning.

Her child part needed to feel connected, loved, and safe with others. Her greatest fear was to be abandoned and left unprotected. Anne's teenage part needed to know that she mattered to others, because her greatest fear was that she wasn't important. Her adult part needed to know that she wasn't alone in the world and that her feelings were valid. She believed that she would never be understood, protected, and loved (just like her child self). So, as one big "internal family," she experienced great conflict between the different "family members" because their roles, needs, and fears often collided and produced great anxiety for her. She wants to be loved (child), but she is afraid of being rejected (teen), so she takes control of her relationships by not allowing others to get close (adult). This pattern perpetuates her loneliness and inability to connect with others, which is what she truly desires.

Our internal conflicts are evident by the quality of our external relationships. So, essentially, our internal conflicts become self-fulfilling prophecies because the very thing that troubles our mind is the very thing we end up creating in our external relationships, as Anne did. This internal conflict can even affect our spiritual relationship with God. We want to trust and depend wholeheartedly in God, but because we have been disappointed one too many times, we'd rather just not get our hopes up. Does this sound familiar? This creates tension within ourselves because we believe that He is trustworthy—after all, His Word says so—but the fear of disappointment holds us hostage and prohibits us from living a life free from the need to be in control and know all things.

OUR NEED FOR ATTACHMENT WITH OTHERS

When our bodies have physically matured but we haven't dealt with our childhood attachment injuries, we end up with stunted internal growth. That little child within us will forever be small and timidly balled up in a corner until we take the time to learn about his or her needs and fears and reconnect at the place he or she was wounded.

Revisiting these childhood wounds are never comfortable because they leave us feeling vulnerable and exposed. This can produce all kinds of emotions in us, ranging from anger to intense grief. This process feels pretty close to having a bandage ripped off a fresh cut on your arm. Although the wound is deep and painful, the only way it will heal is if we expose it, give it the proper care, and allow it to go through the proper healing process. When this happens, you may feel like you are reliving the very moment your attachment with others was severed. When our attachment,[6] our bond with others, is injured, we can develop one of the three insecure attachment styles: **anxious**, **dismissive-avoidant**, or **fearful-avoidant.**[7] An attachment injury is when somebody does (or doesn't) say or do something to you and it changes the way you connect with others and with yourself as a result. For example, if you were never told that you were loved, then as an adult, you may avoid relationships because you believe that nobody will love you.

Anxious Attachment

An anxious attachment develops when parents are inconsistently responsive to the child's needs. For example, the mother may respond to the child's cries, then ignore the child's cries. The child grows to be anxious and often seeks approval and comfort from others in order to feel worthy. They often have a positive view of others, but a negative view of self. They are "clingers" who are overly emotionally dependent on others and hold on for dear life not to be abandoned. Although clingy, they may also present as very demanding and bossy when they feel there is a threat to their attachment with you. So their thought process may be, *If you spend time away from me, then you are neglecting me; thus, you don't really love me. I must not be good enough, so in order for me to feel like you love me, you must do XYZ.*

Avoidant Attachments

Then you have the avoidant-attached people. These individuals most likely had parents who were not very responsive at all to their needs; therefore, they learned to detach from the need to connect or feel their emotions. The parent's unresponsiveness can either be intentional or unintentional, yet it still has the same effect on the child. For example, a single mother of three may be very unresponsive to her children's emotional needs, but only because she is working three jobs trying to feed them.

Dismissive-avoidant individuals do not seek emotional attachment often, and when they do, they can easily detach from it. They often reject love and appear very nonchalant when it comes to relationships. They are compulsively self-reliant and their view of self is often positive while their view of others is often negative. It is not that they do not need love; instead, their behaviors can be seen as defenses that protect them from getting hurt. So their thought process may be, *In order to prevent you from hurting me, I just won't let you get close to me."*

Fearful-avoidant individuals are uncertain about how to get their needs met. They want to be close, but they are also afraid of getting too close. These individuals are often on emotional roller coasters, experiencing high "highs" and low "lows" in their relationships. They will approach and avoid love all at the same time. So their thought process may be, *I want you to love me, but you probably will hurt me, so I am confused as to whether I should come close or back away.*

Secure Attachment

The desired goal is to build a **secure attachment style,** which can be done even if you have had an insecure attachment style the majority of your life. A secure attachment style starts with parents who are warm, nurturing, supportive, and responsive to the child's needs. The child feels secure within herself and also trusts that her parents are safe and loving people. Secure people have a positive view of others and of self; they are comfortable with being vulnerable and transparent. They are also comfortable with being connected while, at the same time, OK with autonomy. They are accepting of their flaws and are not self-critical. So their thought process may be, *I am comfortable loving you because I trust that you have my best interest in mind and I know that I can come to you for support when I am distressed.*

If a secure attachment style was never formed with the caregiver, then adults can form "earned secure attachments" by building relationships with securely-attached people (including the therapist). It is interesting to note that we can have a mixture of all of these in one relationship, and we can also have different attachment styles depending on the relationship that we are referring to. For example, you can have an anxious attachment with your mom, an avoidant-dismissive attachment with your dad, an anxious attachment with your spouse, and a secure attachment with your therapist.

I believe it is very beneficial to know what our "go to" or default attachment style is when under stress, emotionally overwhelmed, or threatened. Knowing your attachment style will help you know what your typical defense strategies are. It is a great starting point to know this so that you can begin working towards minimizing your unhealthy defenses and building a secure attachment. You can find various attachment questionnaires online.[8]

Main Take Away Point

Your past does not solely determine your future but it is a huge contributing factor to the outcome of your present and your future.

Free Training Video
Visit www.trillionsmall.com/book-traumaeffects
for a free training on this chapter.

CHAPTER TWO

THE CARRYOVER EFFECTS OF CHILDHOOD ATTACHMENT INJURIES INTO ADULTHOOD

THE SAME SYMPTOMS EXPERIENCED in childhood have a high probability of carrying over into adulthood if an intervention is not put in place. The following are other coping mechanisms the child may develop and carry into adulthood (or develop as an adult). This is by no means an exhaustive list of all the possibilities, but it represents the common ones:

Negative view of self and/or others

As discussed in the previous chapter, insecurely-attached individuals can develop a negative view of self, others, or both. A negative view of others can be characterized by low trust and fear of others along with an irrational belief that all people are unsafe. A negative view of self can be characterized by low self-trust, low self-esteem, low self-worth, high self-hatred, and high self-criticism along with an irrational belief that the self is bad, unworthy, dirty, and other similar negative cognitions.

Scripture reminds us that we are fearfully and wonderfully made in the image of God. Since we are to be like God, we should not only love ourselves but love others as well (Ps. 139:14; Gen. 1:27; Mark 12:31).

Compulsive Self-Reliance

This is often seen in avoidantly attached individuals who have an intense need for control. It is often rooted in low trust in others. Poor delegation abilities also inhibit relationships/partnerships from forming because of an "I'll do it myself" mentality. Being compulsively self-reliant often places you in a place of self-induced isolation because others are seen as irrelevant and the self (ego) is elevated. It also seems to boil down to a safeguard against disappointments from others.

Scripture reminds us that we are to work together with God and fellowship in community with one another (I Cor. 3:9; Heb. 10:25).

Maladaptive Perfectionism

Not all perfectionism is bad. Adaptive perfectionistic people strive for excellence but also give themselves some slack if need be and are OK with imperfections. Maladaptive perfectionistic[1] people, on the other hand, are never satisfied with their work. Research suggests a correlation between maladaptive perfectionism and high parental expectations, criticism, and responsiveness based on the child's performance. As a result, they set high, sometimes unrealistic, goals that can be detrimental to their health. Such high standards may also be negatively correlated with low self-compassion especially if the individual thinks that self-compassion means being comfortable with low standards (which it is not).

Even if they meet their goals, they still find it hard to celebrate because they feel they could have done better. Soon after that goal is complete, they spend little time, if any, celebrating and soon they will be in search of the next project/challenge to perfect. Maladaptive perfectionists seek self-worth in the fulfillment of such high standards. Because of these high standards, you may find that procrastination is perfectionism's nearest cousin. This is due, in part, to the thought process that says, *If I can't do it perfectly, then I won't do it at all.*

Scripture reminds us that God *does* desire for us to be perfect (Greek: *teleios*[2]), but we must know that this word is used to mean fully mature/grown and having complete development or reaching the end of a goal. God desires for us all to have excellent Christian character (Matt. 5:48; James 1:4).

Shame

Individuals who are high in maladaptive perfectionism rarely recognize that they have an underlying layer of shame. At the slightest hint of failure, a seed of shame is planted. This is due to one's identity being tied to what they DO instead of who they BE. Pardon the incorrect grammar, but shame and perfectionism are also first cousins, because if I do not DO good, then I must not BE good, and in order to BE good, I must DO, and if I can't do, then shame begins to grow and diminish my self-worth. This especially can be challenging for men who feel they can't provide for the family.

Shame often goes unnoticed because perfectionism keeps you so busy that you do not deal with what is beneath the surface. In order to learn who we "be," we must seize from what we "do" long enough to see. Learning to "be" simply means accepting one's self despite the works that you do and learning to revel in rest.

Scripture reminds us that before we ever DID anything, God chose and accepted us. We know that when we get too busy doing and not being, He makes us rest from doing, just like He did (Jer. 1:5; Ps. 23:2; Gen. 2:2).

Fear

Many times we are unaware of our fears. The underlying fears are usually the factors that keep our engines running to near exhaustion. You can have the fear of failure, rejection, being alone, not being good enough, being abandoned, not being loved, losing control, and even the unknown. Our fears can either immobilize us or push us to the place of maladaptive behaviors, such as maladaptive perfectionism, people pleasing, and obsessive-compulsive behaviors, in order to find a sense of control.

You can fill in the blank to the following statement and discover the driving force of your actions (or lack thereof). First, think of something that you do but you really don't want to or something that you don't do, but you want to. Then ask yourself what is the worst that could happen if you do or don't do it, then fill in the blanks. "If I do/do not _____ then I fear_____ (what may happen?). For example, "If I do not say yes to all of your requests then I fear you will be mad and reject me." Or, "If I do step out on faith, I fear that I will fail." If what you choose to do (or don't do) is rooted in fear and not rooted in power, love, and a sound mind (sound judgment), then it may be time to self-evaluate and make any necessary adjustments.

Scripture reminds us that fear is a spirit and God is not the one who has placed that inside of us (2 Tim. 1:7).

Egocentrism

In individualistic cultures, the "self" seems to be what is elevated versus the "we" of the society. Our first inclination is to express how we feel, what we think, and what we would do, but in order to step away from our egos, we must learn to intuit other's feelings, thoughts, and motives. It takes practice, initiative, and intentionality to see through the eyes of someone else. Without this capability, we will be stuck in a self-centered, self-fulfilling, and selfish mindset that robs us from fully maturing. Children are this way; it is all about *them*. If something good happens, it is because of them; if something bad happens, it is also because of them.

This phenomenon explains why children often think that their parent's divorce was their fault. This can carry over into adulthood and cause us to think that if something is messed up or if we do something to make someone mad, then we must have done something wrong. We may go a step further and think that something must be wrong with us because it is all about ME and what I could have done to prevent or change it. This is very apparent with codependents who feel that it is their fault that their loved one is a sex addict or an alcoholic.

I remember when God first revealed to me that I was still immature in this area. I was actually shocked because I didn't see myself as self-centered and self-absorbed, but I was. Mainly because I was still operating from a dismissive-avoidant attachment, and I thought I was all good and others were all bad (for the most part), especially people who I felt rejected me. Once I stepped out of my egocentric mindset, I was able to see from other's perspectives and understand that just because they didn't return my phone call or text didn't mean they rejected me or were ignoring me; it simply meant that they were busy and forgot—nothing more and nothing less.

Scripture reminds us to be humble and to consider others before ourselves. Selfishness only leads to chaos in every area of our life because it is an evil and unspiritual practice. We instead should center our lives around peace, deference, purity, and other good fruits (Phil. 2:3-4; James 3:13-18).

Low Ability to Regulate Emotions

It can be very difficult managing your emotions when you have experienced a childhood attachment injury. One of the purposes of an attachment to a caregiver is to help the child self-soothe until he or she learns how to do it on their own. The idea of regulating intense emotions can seem almost foreign when the child never learned how to self-soothe. When children cannot internally regulate their emotions, they turn to external "soothing" behaviors such as pulling their hair, banging their heads, and throwing tantrums. If we have a low capacity to regulate our emotions as adults, we may not literally roll out on the floor screaming but, internally, our emotions are running all over the place.

Being able to regulate your emotions begins with developing a self-soothing strategy to help ground you. This can be done through mindfulness practice, mediation, and yoga. Also, you must allow yourself to sit in the uncomfortable emotions so that you can begin to build a tolerance and acceptance for them.

Scripture reminds us that practicing self-control is a way to regulate our emotions. God also reminds us that He cares enough to comfort us, and He is big enough to handle all of our emotions and cares of the world (Gal. 5:23, 2 Cor. 1:3-5; 1 Pet. 5:7).

Impulsivity

Being impulsive can derive from the need to be in control and the inability to regulate your own emotions. Often, impulsive decisions are emotional decisions, rooted in anxiety. Very little, if any, thought or planning is put into it. As a child you probably acted without thinking about it, and that was acceptable.

But if you are stuck in that childhood state developmentally due to trauma, you probably do the same thing as an adult. An example would be a woman constantly getting in and out of bad relationships in order to fill some sort of void. Another example would be someone sending you a mean text/email and your first impulse is to respond immediately and "give him or her a piece of your mind."

Personally, I find it very tempting to be impulsive when I am experiencing too much emotional stimuli. If I am overwhelmed with joy about an opportunity, I can make an impulsive decision. I can also do the same if I am very anxious and uncomfortable. Doing so seems to help me rid myself of the uncomfortable feelings.

God shared with me that impulsive people are like wide receivers who gather in the huddle to hear the next play, and as soon as they all yell, "break," someone sprints down the field before everyone else had a chance to line up, before the quarterback even yelled "hike." As Christians we must learn to be patient and wait on God's timing so that we are not penalized for getting ahead of Him.

Scripture reminds us that impulsive and hasty decisions cause us to miss the mark and step out of God's will. They also cause us to say foolish things we often regret shortly thereafter. We must sit down and consider what we are going to say and do before we actually do it. It is clear that we should not be anxious for anything. Moses also teaches us that impulsivity that is rooted in angry impatience

can cause us to miss God's promises for us. But we can take comfort in knowing that if we pray, listen, and believe, He will guide us (Prov. 19:2, 29:20; Luke 14:28-30; Phil. 4:6; Num. 20:10-12, 9:8; John 10:27; Isa. 28:16; Ps. 23:3).

Rumination

If you have ever found yourself dwelling on who, what, when, where, and how in relation to something that happened to you, then you have been an active participator in rumination. Rumination literally takes over our mental space and floods us with a seemingly endless amount of thoughts. It can get so bad that your thoughts begin to generalize into areas of your life that were not a part of the original trauma. For example, imagine the thoughts that would run through a ten-year-old's head as he waits hours at the bus stop for his mom to come pick him up, especially after finding out that she has forgotten about him. He may not have the vocabulary for it then, but that experience would probably leave him feeling rejected, unimportant, and forgotten about.

Now, as an adult, if anybody is even five minutes late for a meeting, his mind goes from zero to one hundred, thinking and feeling the same things he felt as that ten-year-old forgotten little boy. The thoughts are so all-consuming that even when his date shows up one minute later, the entire night is ruined because his brain has already prepped and primed his mind and body for rejection. So even though he wasn't rejected, his mind and body respond as if the rejection has already happened.

Scripture reminds us to cast all of our cares onto God and to transform our lives by transforming our minds. A way to begin doing this is by not dwelling on the past, and thinking about things that are positive (I Pet. 5:7; Rom. 12:2; Phil. 3:13, 4:8).

Dissociation

Dissociation is your brain essentially going offline emotionally, mentally, and physically. Mild dissociation is common among most of us. Examples would be driving home from work and not remembering much of the drive; reading a page in a book only to realize you don't recall anything you just read; or sitting in a lecture hall, daydreaming. There are other forms of dissociation that may be more overwhelming and chronic; these often require clinical treatment. The more severe forms of dissociation may be due to psychological trauma. They can range from dissociative amnesia (forgetting all or parts of the traumatic experience) to dissociative identity disorder (actually splitting off into different personality alters), which was formerly known as multiple personality disorder.

Specific experiences of dissociating can be feelings of floating, feeling foggy, blurred vision, mentally blacking out, people and/or things appearing further away than they actually are, feeling detached from your body, and feeling like the experience isn't real. Some of us may dissociate and are unaware of it; or, we are aware of it, but uncertain of the cause. I recall my vision getting very foggy with one client in particular. It didn't happen with the client before or after her, so I discussed it with my supervisor to make sense of it. I discovered that the look she was giving me was one that was familiar. Her look of desperation and fear triggered my own stuff.

When we dissociate, it is as if our brain turns its "head," closes its "eyes," and cover its "ears" as it braces itself for the blow of the uncomfortable and maybe even traumatic experience. This very well could be the case with men who withdraw in emotionally-charged situations. He may not be rejecting you. Turning away from you instead of toward you when you are hurting may be the only way he knows how to deal with intense emotions. *This is why it is important for us to know how we cope with different things in life.* If dissociating is your primary way of coping, it's helpful to become self-aware to know what causes you to dissociate and to know when you are in the moment so that you can use grounding techniques (such as deep breathing) to bring you back to the room.

Scripture reminds us that we no longer have to live the old way that destroys us but that we can live a new life that gives us freedom from bondage. God tells us to give Him our overwhelming load and He will carry it (Eph. 4:22-24; Gal. 5:1; 2 Cor. 3:17; Matt. 11:28-30).

Fight, Flight, or Freeze Modes

These are the three common responses to a threat. It is the brain's way of keeping us safe and getting us away from danger. If we feel we are in danger, our brain will either equip us to fight or run, and if we can't do either, then we do nothing and freeze. When faced with danger, a child isn't strong enough to fight back nor fast enough to get away, so their response is often to freeze and dissociate (i.e., thinking of something happy or separating from themselves in the moment). As adults, fighting or running does become a viable option, but there are still times where freezing is the only option. You're like a deer in the headlights; you know you are in danger, but you can't fight the "car." You are immobilized by fear, so you just stand there, paralyzed. We often freeze when we feel powerless and helpless.

When you are in *fight* mode, you could respond with clinched fists or jaw, anger, an aggressive tone of voice, increased heart rate, or the desire to hit. When you are in *flight* mode, you may feel anxious, restless, tense, or short of breath. When you are in *freeze* mode, you could experience, body sensations such as shallow breathing or feeling stuck, heavy, or numb. It is beneficial to recognize these symptoms (and others) because they provide you with insight about how safe you are feeling. You can experience more than one of these responses with a single incident. For example, you could be arguing with your significant other (fight), but as time passes you find yourself giving up (freeze) and eventually desiring to just get away from them (flight).

I experienced both freezing and the desire to flee while on a canoe trip with my brother. Everything was fine until a snake about three feet long began swimming toward my end of the canoe like he was about to strike me! I immediately panicked, dropped my paddle, turned my back to the snake (as if that would make it leave me alone), and started screaming at the top of my lungs. As I was screaming, the thought crossed my mind to jump in the water (that would have been smart right?!), but just as I was about to jump in, I heard a big splat. My brother went into fight mode, unlike me, and took his paddle and hit the snake. The thought never crossed my mind to use my paddle, but I'm glad it crossed my brother's! It just goes to show that we can do and think very irrational things when in the face of trauma (i.e., a child thinking it is his fault his parents are fighting). There are times when we need to fight or run, and there are times when we do not. With increased awareness and practice, we can learn to stay present when there's no need to run; we can learn to take action when doing nothing (freezing) hurts others; and we can learn to stay calm when there's no need to fight back.

Scripture reminds us that God is there to help us when we are in trouble and that we do not have to fear because He is always with us (Ps. 46:1; Deut. 31:6).

Silent Anger

This type of anger can slowly eat away at you internally if you allow it to. It may be hard to put your finger on silent anger because it is often nonverbal and/or indiscernible by the untrained eye. It doesn't lash out with piercing words nor does it throw things across the room; it just sits and brews deep within, often unnoticed even by the one who is silently angry. Silent anger is the type of anger that feels it doesn't have a right or reason to be expressed. Or, silently angry people may feel they have the right to be angry, but they do not have a safe place to express it. I find this very common when the anger is directed toward a parent.

I personally never would have considered myself angry until I went through the EMDR training. When it came time for me to be the "client" while practicing in our small groups, I became very irritated with both the process and the memories that were coming up. I was so irritated that I didn't want to continue the process. The small group facilitator noticed my agitation and asked one question that made me break down in tears. She asked, "When did you learn that you had to hold in your anger?" That simple but penetrating question struck me to my core, because in all of my years of living, I never knew I was holding in so much anger. I assume I learned at an early age that anger was bad or that bad things happened when people were angry, so I presume I learned to keep it all in. I was able to release my anger when I gave voice to my experiences and stopped minimizing its effects on my life.

Scripture reminds us that if we are angry, we shouldn't allow it to cause us to sin or give room for Satan to come into our life. Thus, we must control ourselves by being wise and slow to anger. Anger doesn't bring about the righteous life that God desires, so we need to deal with it before it destroys

us. Although it may be difficult, we must be compassionate and forgiving toward those who have hurt us (Eph. 4:26-27; Prov. 29:11; James 1:19-20; Eccles. 7:9; Col. 3:8).

Fear of Compassion/Closeness from Others

If fear of being close to others and receiving love and care from them could speak, it would say, *If I let you close to me then I have to become vulnerable/ transparent, and if I do that, I risk you seeing my flaws and imperfections that I am ashamed of. If I allow you to see those parts of me, then I risk you rejecting me, which will only reaffirm my fears. So, instead of going through all of that, I will just keep you at arm's length and play it safe.* A majority of this fear has to do with the defenses that were just mentioned.

When children have childhood attachment injuries, their attachment system is thrown off balance and needs to be recalibrated. When the system is being recalibrated, it may have some push back and resistance to it, especially if it is used to not being loved and cared for. It is as if closeness is a virus, and the tainted attachment system is the white blood cells destroying anything that gets close. It takes time and a sense of safety with a person in order to reopen that attachment system which was shut down as a child.

Scripture reminds us that the Lord is close to the brokenhearted, and if we get closer to Him, He will get closer to us in return (Ps. 34:18; James 4:8).

Low Self-Compassion

Not only can we lack the ability to accept compassion from others, we can also have a difficult time being compassionate toward ourselves. It is true; we often are our biggest critics, and if we could have ourselves arrested, it would be for aggravated assault to the self with an internal weapon. When others aren't very loving toward us as a child, we internalize that and begin to treat ourselves the same way others treat us. We are not born self-critics, so this is a learned behavior. It is also important to note that maladaptive perfectionists are often low in self-compassion because they are so self-critical and harsh to themselves. Self-compassion will be discussed in more detail in chapter 4.

Scripture reminds us that God comforts us and has compassion for us when He sees that we are lost, wounded, and sick. And since we are to love others as we love ourselves, we must learn to love ourselves, because we are not to hate others (2 Cor. 1:3-4; Matt. 6:34, 9:36, 14:14; Mark 12:31).

Unhealthy Relationships

Interestingly enough, I have noticed that individuals who have low self-compassion often experience more unhealthy relationships than those who are more self-compassionate. As previously discussed, childhood attachment injuries affects the way the child bonds with others as well as himself. If he developed an insecure attachment as a child, he is likely to have an insecure attachment as an adult. This type of attachment results in unhealthy relationships due, in part, to relational hypervigilance, specifically for anxiously-attached individuals. Relational hypervigilance will also be discussed more in chapter 5.

Scripture reminds us to build healthy relationships by making amends and peace as often as we can (Matt. 5:23; Rom. 12:18; Heb. 12:14).

Walls

Everything that we have mentioned up to this point can be considered part of your wall. The walls we put up in life are made up of several bricks. Each brick represents a defense or a barrier that either blocks/protects us from receiving something or hides a part of us that we don't want to be exposed. For example, anger can be used as a defense that blocks us from understanding others, and it hides the fact that we are fearful of being rejected. Unwillingness to be vulnerable can be a barrier that hides our flaws and imperfections from others and prevents us from forming relationships based on truth and honesty. Another example is compulsive self-reliance. This can be both a defense and a barrier. It protects us from having to depend on others and risk the chance of being disappointed or hurt by them. It also blocks us from enjoying community and fellowship with others, which puts us in a place of isolation. It hides the fact that we really *do* desire to have people near but are fearful of closeness. It's a lonely mindset because the only reason you can't hurt me is because I won't let you get close to me in the first place.

This may be quite paradoxical, but I have found that we become more defensive when our defenses begin to wear off. When your cover is blown, you have to become more defensive to guard your soft, vulnerable spots. It's like having a breach in security; now the whole army has to come out. Our defenses begin to wear off over time when our minds and bodies grow weary of being on a 24/7 watch. I noticed myself becoming much more angry and defensive when God began to challenge me to drop my mask and be whom He called me to be, which was authentic and vulnerable. It wasn't that I was mad at God, but I was mad that I could no longer use my aggressive, nonchalant, blunt, compulsively self-reliant responses when relating to people anymore. That was how I had been for so long, so when He asked me to change, it was like He was asking me to give up my protection and sense of safety.

He wanted me to give up my false sense of security and learn to trust in His true hand of protection. My defenses were essentially saying, "God I can handle this on my own!" Although uncomfortable and scary, I began to slowly knock down my walls, brick by brick. I did it because I knew it was for my emotional, spiritual, mental, and physical health. Being defensive is exhausting! We aren't designed to walk around with the weight of all our bricks. We are meant to be more like Iron Man,[3] knowing when it is appropriate to put on our armor and be on guard . . . and when it is safe to take it off.

Scripture reminds us that we don't have to defend ourselves because He will do that for us. He will protect us and let no weapon formed against

us prosper. God wants our walls to be torn down so that His light and glory will shine through us for the world to see. That can't be done with our walls of defense up (Rom. 12:19; Ps. 27; Isa. 54:17; Luke 11:33).

❤

As I began searching Scripture for understanding and solutions to each of these carryover effects of childhood attachment injuries, I discovered that most of these ways of coping are either unspiritual or actually sin. When we behave in any of these ways, we are not representing the image of God, which is missing the mark. Although the resulting effects may have evolved from your trauma experiences, which were not your fault at all, how you choose to respond and live your life after the fact is your responsibility. If we do not deal with the aftereffects of trauma, we can give the enemy a foot into our lives and he will attempt to keep us in bondage by putting these obstacles in our way (or by helping us to create our *own* obstacles). These obstacles make it difficult for us to walk out a pure and righteous life the way God intended.

How It Feels To Be Hurt By Others

I was curious as to how others describe their experiences being hurt by others, so I asked several friends and family the following question: "If you could sum up your experiences of being hurt by people in two to three words (in any capacity . . . physically, emotionally, mentally, spiritually, etc.), what would those words be?" Here is the list:

Growing Pains
Distrust/Broken Trust*
Insecurity
Anxious
Despondent
Taken for Granted
Shattered Hopes
Abyss
Disbelief
Gut-wrenching
Confronted
Broken
Speechless
Empty
Used
Pain
Backstabbed
Hurt
Mad/Angry*

Disappointment*
Future Distress
Revenge
Low Self-Esteem
Sad
Agonizing
Confused*
Hopeless
Shut Down
Anguish
Numb
Betrayal*
Never Ending Story
Thrown Aside
Alone/Lonely*
Unexpected
Delusion
Rejection

Indicates those that were most common

There were also some positive responses. These could have been responses immediately after the hurt or they could have been post-healing from the hurt.

Thank You, Lord
Test of Faith

It's All Good
Made Me Stronger

Transformative	No Regrets
I Forgive You	Informative
Life Goes On	Pray for Them

As I read each response, I could relate to each one, as you also may. Although I only asked a small number of people, I still believe that if I were to ask every human being in the world the same question, there would still be national consensus confirming that being hurt by others hurts us in more ways than one! This is even apparent in the quantity and intensity of the symptoms mentioned above, which wasn't even an exhaustive list of all possible carryover effects.

Main Take Away Point

The ways in which you think, feel, and act today are simply reflections of the various things that you have encountered in life. Involving the good, the bad, and the ugly stuff.

Free Training Video
Visit www.trillionsmall.com/book-carryovereffects for a free training on this chapter.

CHAPTER THREE

THE CYCLE OF CHILDHOOD ABUSE

AS A COUNSELOR I have heard many people's stories. Many of those stories centered around abuse, whether physical, sexual, or psychological. While listening, I kept noticing some very common patterns. Many of my clients' presenting problems (past or present) were exactly the same, or similar, experiences that their parents had had with their parents (my clients' grandparents). This is not always the case, of course, because there are amazing stories of new parents making a stand and not doing to their children what was done to them.

WHEN BEING IN THE FAMILY GETS HEAVY

I'd like to call these common family patterns "weighted links," which is the passing on of maladaptive habits, behaviors, cognitions, and affects that keep us imprisoned. Each generation passes on a new link that continues to form into heavier and heavier chains. From a spiritual perspective, we often call these generational curses. However, since Ezekiel 18:14-20 says that we are no longer punished for our father's sins, I will save that debate for another day. But here's some food for thought: Let's say that a father and son practice the same sin and both are punished for their sins. Does that mean God punished the son because of the dad or did God punish the son because of his own sin? Is that a generational curse issue or a choice issue?

Moving on . . .

Weighted links can be related to emotional, spiritual, mental, physical, and behavioral problems that seem to "run" in the family. For example, think about when a grandfather, father, and son all struggle with alcohol and aggressive problems; when many of the family members struggle with diabetes and obesity; when a grandmother, mother, and daughter all have been married two, three, and four times to what seems to be the same type of men; when everybody in the family has trust issues; or when many people in the family are depressed or anxious (yes, this can be genetic, but not always). The list can go on and on. What persistent struggles "run" in your house that you may have linked into?

It could be possible that your parent's fears and worries were not just contagious and you caught them; you could be dealing with a deeply-rooted family tree matter that could have spiritual implications, or not. Maybe you are not up against a demon who keeps making you gain weight; maybe you are up against a Double Whopper with fries, chocolate chip cookies, doughnuts, honeybuns, cinnamon rolls, ice cream, fried chicken, and pork chops with macaroni and cheese, anti-healthy-eating-and-avoiding-sweat-because-you-don't-want-to-mess-up-your-hair kind of "demon." But what do I know?

Moving on again . . .

REVELATION LIFTS WEIGHTS

I have helped many of my clients discover that some of the weight they were carrying was related to what their grandparents and parents were also carrying. If I discern that this weighted-link phenomena is present, I simply ask, "Whose stuff is this that you are dealing with?" That is actually a really good EMDR "interweave" (for clinicians) for clients who feel overwhelmed with their current situation—one that appears to persist from generation to generation. The look on the client's face when they hear that question says it all. It tells me that they have never been asked that question before and have never thought to ask that question of themselves! After the look of deep thought passes, they then feel a great sense of release because they now realize that the weight they have been "carrying" was not all theirs. Then, the third look that often crosses the client's face is one of anger and disgust. These feelings are common after they realize they have been suffering under weight that they didn't have to. The catch to our chains is that we put in our own link as well, which means we have some part in participating in the family pattern. The load becomes easier when we cast everyone else's weight off our plates but understand that we still have the responsibility to tote the load that we contributed.

God has called us to carry each other's burdens. While some of our burdens can be related to sin, others may not be. But Galatians 6:1-2 lets us know that we should have the love and gentle support from other fellow Christian brothers and sisters around us to help in the healing process. Don't try to tackle your chains on your own. I encourage you to seek professional help from a therapist as well as from loving and supportive family and friends as you go through the process.

It is a very freeing moment when you realize that your sadness, anger, anxiety, addictions, and other habits can be broken simply by breaking off chains that have been formed and wrapped around your life. That doesn't mean that the process will be easy, but it does provide hope. I believe God is strong enough to free us from bondage, just as He did for Paul and Silas in Acts 16:26.

THE CYCLE

As we have discussed, we all have unique stories with different scripts, plots, and characters, but the themes and the patterns are pretty similar. Figure 1 illustrates the cycle of childhood abuse. This is a cyclical and not linear pattern, because debating whether the chicken or the egg comes first would be an interminable discussion.

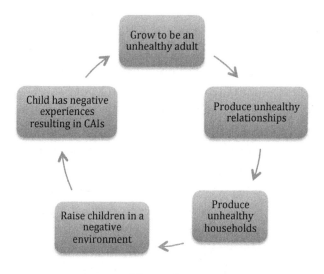

Figure 1
(CAIs = Childhood Attachment Injuries)

As you see from the diagram, this is not a Vegas cycle where "what happens at homes stays at home." No, what happens at home manifests itself outside of the home and has an effect on our thoughts, behaviors, decisions, desires, and emotions. A child who is raised in an unhealthy environment can, in turn, either internalize or externalize what he or she has experienced. For example, a child can turn inward and become very self-critical because of her environment, or she can turn outward and have various behavior problems, such as being defiant and unruly. Let's discuss the cycle a bit further.

What Happens to the Child

As children, we need to be seen, heard, and attached/connected with. As adults, we have the same needs. I love the story of Leah, found in Genesis 29:31-35. It is a perfect example that represents the needs we have and the great lengths we will go to in order to fulfill them. To make a long story short, Leah was married to Jacob and she was in "competition" with his other wife, Rachel, who he liked much more. Rachel also happened to be Leah's sister. Leah could have children, but Rachel couldn't, so Leah tried to use that to her advantage. It didn't work. She had her first child and thought surely her husband would *see* her, so she named him Reuben. But he didn't. She then had her second child and thought surely her husband would *hear* her, so she named him Simeon. But he still didn't. She then had her third child and thought surely her husband would be *attached* to her, so she named him Levi. But after three children, Jacob still didn't meet any of her needs, so she had one more child and decided to let God meet all of her needs. She named the child Judah, for she praised the Lord.

If you can't relate to Leah, then maybe you can relate to Rachel, who, although loved, still had needs that were not met, as she grieved being barren in her womb. No matter what our presenting problem is, I have discovered that, at our core, we all often have the exact same desire—the desire to be known by others and to be loved. When a child doesn't feel known or loved in his first interactions with people in the world, it has major implications on the child's views of himself, others, the world around him, and even God.

What Happens in the Child

If these basic needs are not met (beyond food and shelter), we experience attachment injuries that begin to pile up. Recall that these injuries affect the way we experience self and others. Many adults who experienced these injuries learned to either suppress or compartmentalize their feelings to avoid being inundated with their emotions. Each can encourage the use of different external behaviors to numb, avoid, and get rid of "negative" emotions, such as sadness, fear, and anxiety. Examples of external behaviors are becoming a workaholic, relying on others' feelings to know how to feel, and participating in self-injurious behaviors such as cutting. Drug and alcohol use or abuse is also common.

If the child begins to question the validity and importance of her emotions, then she soon will either become hypo-aroused and hardly be moved by emotional stimuli or she will become hyper-aroused and feel way too much of her feelings. Both of these are on the extreme ends of the spectrum. If the child never learned how to regulate and cope with her emotions, it will be difficult for her to stay in the middle of the two, which is where we want to be emotionally.

Not only is our affect altered, our cognitions are as well. Trauma often causes us to feel like we are bad, dirty, used goods, not worthy, unlovable, not good enough, or unimportant. It also often causes us to feel unsafe, unprotected, and exposed.

What Happens Through the Child

We generalize. After the abuse has occurred and the internal damage is done, what is on the inside will now move through the child into his or her world. For example, during a group counseling session, I noticed that one of the members rarely spoke. I was interested in knowing more about her unwillingness or apprehension about speaking, so I met with her individually. In our individual meeting, I learned that her living situation was not the best, emotionally. She shared that her dad often told her to shut up when she started talking thus her reluctance to open up during group. She stated that she figured if her dad didn't want to hear what she had to say, then nobody else did. Her dad's verbal abuse toward her caused her to internalize the irrational belief that her voice didn't matter. As a result, she based her life around that lie and chose to keep quiet.

What we see in this case is how we can predict how others will respond to us based on how others have responded to us in the past. This mindset can actually do more harm than good due to the possibility of inaccurate predictions. So, if a child was slapped often after he made his dad mad, then when you frown at him in the same way his dad did, his brain automatically thinks a slap will follow. Or let us consider a woman who experienced her father walking out on her and her mom at a young age. When her husband tells her that he wants to take a walk to clear his mind, she isn't thinking he just needs some air, she's probably fearing he won't come back.

I know that for me, there were times when I was fearful of investing too much into people because I felt that they would either leave me or that I would end up having to leave them. I know I had this same fear as a child because I still have a book that I wrote when I was in the third grade, and there were many references to the fear of being left behind (See appendix A to read the book). As you can imagine, it becomes very easy to generalize our past onto our present, misinterpret other's motives, and even ruin new moments of opportunity to live and learn.

We withdraw. When our past is present, we begin to dig a deep well and place ourselves in it. This is "The mall is open, but nobody is shopping" phenomena. This doesn't mean that you are mentally slow. It means that your body is here in the present, but you are totally disconnected from the people and things around you. So when people go to search for you, they can't find you. This produces frustration in them because they want you to show them who you are. What they fail to realize is that you can't show them who you are because you don't even know who you are. You think you "lost" who you were a long time ago, never realizing that you can't lose you. However, when this occurs, your frustration and urge to withdraw increases, causing you to sink even deeper in the well.

Although you have dug yourself deep in this well, you managed to come out long enough to get into a relationship or marriage and have children. Your children do not understand that you are still dealing with your childhood issues, so they are now getting the same ill treatment your parents gave you (also probably because of unresolved trauma). Hurt people hurt people, intentionally or unintentionally, and this is what perpetuates the cycle of childhood abuse.

MAIN TAKE AWAY POINT

Others may have caused you hurt as a child but now that you are an adult you must heal and break the cycle or you will begin to inflict internal and external hurt to yourself and eventually to those around you.

Free Training Video
Visit www.trillionsmall.com/book-thecycle
for a free training on this chapter.

CHAPTER FOUR

BREAKING THE CYCLE OF CHILDHOOD ABUSE WITH SELF-COMPASSION

WHAT IS IT ABOUT Jesus and wells? They are often discussed throughout the Bible. Here I'd like to zoom in on two in particular: the well mentioned in Genesis 16 and the well mentioned in John 4.

In Genesis 16 we find the story of the married couple Abram (Abraham) and Sarai (Sarah) and the wife's slave, Hagar. Sarai couldn't get pregnant, so she told her husband to sleep with Hagar. He did and she became pregnant. Hagar began to despise Sarai afterwards. As a result Abram told Sarai to do whatever she wanted to her, so Sarai began mistreating Hagar. Hagar runs away and an angel finds her near a fountain of water in the desert. The angel asks her where she is coming from and where she is going, and Hagar responds that she is running away from her mistress Sarai. The angel tells her to go back, and God will multiple her seed. He also told her that she is to name her son Ishmael because God has heard her affliction. She then says, "You are the God that sees me," so she named that fountain of water (the well) Beer Lahai Roi.

In John 4 we find the story of Jesus' encounter with a Samaritan woman. Jesus was tired on His journey from Judea to Galilee, so He stopped in Samaria and sat down by Jacob's well. Shortly after, a Samaritan woman comes and He asks her to give Him something to drink. She knew he was a Jew, and since Jews did not associate with Samaritans, she became curious as to why He was asking her for some water. Jesus responded, basically saying, "If you knew who I was, you would be asking me for water because you would never thirst again." She is now convinced and asks Him for this water. Very interesting though, Jesus' next response isn't "OK, here is my water"; His next response is "Go get your husband and come back." What makes this request interesting is that she isn't married, although she does have a man around. Let's just say that she has been well acquainted with many other women's husbands and is not highly favored by the wives. The conversation goes on, and eventually she goes back to the town and tells everyone about her encounter with Jesus.

WHAT DOES MY WELL SYMBOLIZE?

A well is a deep, dark hole that contains water but also may contain other foreign objects that are naked to the eye on the surface. When Jesus meets these two women near their well, He is meeting them at the place where they have hidden many things from the surface. The things beneath the surface are often the wounds, scars, and hurts that most people are not aware of. It takes a special internal eye to see them.

Our wells run deep, and some of our wells are running dry. Although the stories may be different, our wells all have symbolic meaning for our pain. For Hagar, the well could have been a place of weariness, fear, trauma, confusion, anger, and isolation. For the Samaritan woman, the well may have been a place of loneliness, rejection, shame, low self-worth, and being taken advantage of.

The beauty in each of these stories is that God spoke directly to their wounds. Their need to be seen, heard, and attached were all met at their well of despair. Not only were these needs met, but the universal core need of needing to be known and loved by others was met as well. Jesus shared specifics about each of their lives with them. He took the time to let them know that He saw them, He heard their cries, He knew what they were going through and what they would become, and He desired to be connected with them in a right relationship.

It didn't matter how deep their well was. A deep well is not indicative of a mission impossible. But it will definitely take effort, intention, and the desire to come out and open yourself up to the healing hands of Jesus to climb out of that well. If we were to reframe the meaning of the deep hole you dug for yourself, I would say that the deeper the well, the more capacity you have, once you and all of your hidden parts are out, to be filled with His living water (John 4:14; 7:38).

THERE WAS COMPASSION AT THE WELL

For these two women, the revitalizing experience at the well did not come until after they had an encounter with God. Once they had an encounter with God, their rough places turned into a place of life: a place of living and a never-ending supply of spiritual water that could quench every last one of their needs far greater than the deepest well full of natural water ever could.

So what did both women encounter that changed their lives forever? They experienced His love and compassion for them! In each story, God showed them love, spoke directly to their needs, and engaged them in a conversation that made them feel connected with Him. Now we do not know whether their encounter with compassion broke the cycle of abuse for them and their children and grandchildren, but from their initial experiences with God, I feel it is safe to assume that those experiences were life-changing, and not just a temporary fix. We can make speculations all day about Ishmael, in particular, considering that the angel told Hagar that he would be an aggressive and hostile man, but what we do know for certain is that these women went back with more than what they had originally. They had a loving compassionate encounter with the Lord, and that changes lives.

INTERNALIZE THE EXPERIENCE AT THE WELL

If God's loving and compassionate encounter with these women changed them, then I'd like to propose that compassion (and for the purposes of this discussion, self-compassion) is a malleable factor to help break the cycle of childhood abuse. I believe that the development of (self) compassion will help to change a person's chaotic internal system (attachment) and shift them from disorder to order. I define a *disordered internal system* as one that has a disruption in the flow due to an infectious disease being present. I define an *ordered internal system* as one that has a disposition that flows and functions with ease. When an infection or blockage occurs in our internal system, we become "dis-eased." The antidote is an element that puts the system at ease, and that element is high dosages of loving self-compassion.

Just look at what one compassionate encounter did for the Samaritan woman. She dropped her water bucket and ran back to where she had come to tell everyone about her experience. Her testimony of how God exposed her past and spoke of her present brought crowds of people to be saved. This moment also teaches us that vulnerability and acceptance of our flaws doesn't cause people to reject us; instead, it draws the right people to us and forms the connections that we desired all along. The Samaritan woman was no longer a thirsty woman, dehydrated and in need of the attention of men; she was now a satisfied woman who brought people to the same well of living water that healed her. She was a breath of fresh air and a cool glass of proverbial water to those who now encountered her.

All throughout Scripture and even today we see how God uses brokenhearted people to turn right back around and heal other brokenhearted people. Jesus tells Simon (Peter) while at the Passover Supper, "Simon, Simon! Indeed, Satan has asked for you, that he may sift you as wheat. But I have prayed for you, that your faith should not fail; and when you have returned to Me, strengthen your brethren" (Luke 22:31-32). Additionally, in Isaiah 61: 4 (NIV), Scripture says that *they* will rebuild the ancient ruins, restore the places long devastated, and renew the ruined cities that have been devastated for generations. For starters, who is *they*? Well, *they* are the people who were described in the previous three verses. *They* are the poor (in spirit and circumstance), the brokenhearted (internal wounds), the captives, the prisoners (who are "blinded" by the darkness), those who mourn, and those who grieve.

SELF-COMPASSION PROVIDES A BUFFER AFTER ABUSE

What Is Self-Compassion

According to Neff (2003),[1] the pioneering researcher in self-compassion, self-compassion has three components: my level of kindness toward myself, my ability to be mindfully self-aware of my experiences and my reactions to my experiences, and my recognition that undesirable circumstances are common to all human beings. In addition, compassion researcher Paul Gilbert defines self-compassion as being able to discern distress and process it rather than avoid it, being able to tolerate distress and painful feelings, being able to intuit the source of your distress and what you need in that moment, and the ability to not be critical and antagonizing about your experiences and behaviors (2005).[2]

I may be mixing variables when I say this, but I believe that love is at the very heart of self-compassion. When you love someone, it hurts to see him or her hurt, so you do what you can to be with them in the pain, and you try your best to ease the pain. When you love someone, you do not intentionally hurt them by being mean and critical; instead, you choose kindness and respect. When you love someone you don't talk to him or her in a rude manner. Second Corinthians 13:4-7 (NIV) reminds us that "Love is patient, love is kind. It does not envy, it does not boast, it is not proud. It does not dishonor others, it is not self-seeking, it is not easily angered, it keeps no record of wrongs. Love does not delight in evil but rejoices with the truth. It always protects, always trusts, always hopes, always perseveres."

I also believe that self-compassion and attachment go hand-in-hand. More specifically, I believe that the primary goal of increasing self-compassion is to build and strengthen a secure self-attachment. The factors that define a secure self-attachment are essentially the same as those for a secure attachment with others. This is the same for self-compassion; compassion can simply be inverted inwardly to make self-compassion.

It mediates my response to my present. How we respond to how others treat us often is a reflection, in part, to our level of self-compassion and security within the self. As an example, if I am secure within myself, then when you criticize my work I don't take it personally because I KNOW that I am good enough and that my work is not a direct reflection of my value as a human being. Contrary to this, if I am not secure in who I am and if I am low in self-compassion, then I begin to take your negative treatment to heart and I begin to internalize it by thinking, *Well, I must have done something wrong if he/she is so mad at me. . . . I'll be perfect next time so this won't happen again. . . . I hope they still think I am good enough.* This point of view is coming from an egocentric state in assuming that if things go awry, then **I** surely must have done something wrong, or **I** surely could've done something to prevent this.

It mediates my response to my past, now. How I respond to my past can directly and indirectly affect those around me. If I have not healed from my past, I will respond to my present the same way I did in my past; which was probably a maladaptive way of coping. So, for example, after your childhood attachment injury you may have learned not to be open with people, to stuff your emotions, and to withdraw when things got too emotionally intense. So, now, when someone asks how you are doing, your first response is "fine," and then you go "hide" in your own silo, internally screaming and crying wishing that somebody could see you. You yearn for the day you can open up and say, "No, I'm not OK," and not have things not fall apart on you when you do (as you imagine will be the case).

It mediates my response to my future. It is pretty difficult to see a bright future through a tainted lens. Our negative childhood experiences give us the tented shades to wear, and we filter our entire lives through them until healing occurs. Everybody and everything that we experience thereafter is seen through our tainted perspective. It isn't until we come across other people with clear lenses that we begin to realize our views could be wrong. The more the "clear-lens people" shine their lights, the more "the tented-lens people" begin to realize that they have been living in the dark.

❤

I do know that all things work together for our good[3], and I also know that our trials make us stronger.[4] I am not denying the fact that these promises are true. Some of you may not like what I am about to say, but sometimes being "too" spiritual prohibits us from getting the proper healing we need. I am not talking about seeking too much prayer, deliverance, and forgiveness. I am talking about those times when we use spirituality to the point that we minimize the fact that people hurt us, and hurt us badly! I was that way. I was stomping around all big and strong saying, "The more you hurt me, the stronger I get, so it doesn't matter . . . I'll be OK," but God showed me that it was a false sense of strength, courage, and healing. It was actually pride. I didn't want to show that people could or had hurt me.

THE GRINCH SYNDROME

How the Grinch Stole Christmas is a perfect movie depicting what happens to us when we have unresolved childhood trauma. The Grinch was psychologically abused by way of bullying. What happened to him in that classroom scarred him for life. What should have been very non-significant turns into his biggest trigger: a razor. The razor experience seemed to be the tipping point of his trauma experience, and when he was faced with it again as an adult, he had the same response that he had as a child, which was mean, aggressive, and vengeful.

Most of us have a Mr. Grinch inside of us. Someone that we truly cared about hurt us and, as a result, we put ourselves into solitary confinement to avoid ever getting hurt again. That is never the case, though. Our walls of protection actually hurt us worse. Mr. Grinch even went as far as hurting himself to avoid the audible reminders of the season that he experienced the most pain in. But here comes Cindy Lou Who, offering him compassion. It truly was her kind-hearted, caring, and considerate nature that helped bring Mr. Grinch to a place of healing. Where his small heart once dwelled, his "new" heart emerged, one full of love and joy.

BREAKING THE CYCLE

Figure 2 illustrates how embedding self-compassion in the cycle can break the cycle of childhood abuse. It can be inserted at any point in the cycle for prevention or intervention. I'd like to focus on the adult who has a childhood attachment injury and is consequently experiencing negative symptomatology.

What follows is my demonstration of the cycle with an attachment-based theoretical foundation. Understanding the cycle of childhood abuse is like understanding the basics of the reproductive system cycle. Self-compassion is the sperm, and the trauma cycle is the egg. Once the self-compassion (the seed) meets the egg, the cycle (menstrual) has to stop and the development of something new has to come about (the baby).

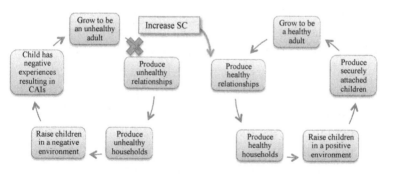

Figure 2
(*CAIs = Childhood Attachment Injuries;*
SC = Self-Compassion)

Self-compassion gives us freedom, and when freedom reigns (rains), it rusts and breaks the chains that have us bound. It helps us form new ways of thinking, feeling, doing, and being. When we as adults begin to increase our self-compassion, we strengthen our inner self. This internal strength provides us with a sense of secure attachment within ourselves. When we feel confident and secure in who we are, we begin to attract similar healthy people into our lives; whereas, before we often attracted people who helped us perpetuate the cycle of childhood abuse. As a healthy couple, we then will be able to create a warm and loving environment for children, which is necessary to the formulation of a secure attachment (with self and others).

Self-compassion can break the cycle of a woman who often sought men who were dismissive and unintentional. An increase in her self-compassion can decrease her tolerance for such maltreatment and increase her self-worth. Self-compassion can also break the cycle of a man who feels that he has to work endless hours to prove to his wife that he is the perfect man worthy of love. An increase in self-compassion can allow him to cut himself some slack if he fails and help him to see that he doesn't have to "do" in order to get the love he needs. Self-compassion is what we all need at our *well of wounds* in order to break our negative cycles.

MAIN TAKE AWAY POINT

The world around us will change when the world within us changes first.

Free Training Video
Visit www.trillionsmall.com/book-selfcompassion
for a free training on this chapter.

CHAPTER FIVE

HOW RELATIONAL HYPERVIGILANCE RELATES TO MY PAST

IN THE PREVIOUS CHAPTER, I illustrated (see figure 2) how childhood attachment injuries can produce unhealthy adult relationships. In this chapter, we will dig deeper to grasp a better understanding of our relationships after a childhood attachment injury.

The pattern of unhealthy relationships is typically well-established long before self-compassion even enters into the picture. It's always interesting to look at the relational patterns of teens and adults with the same childhood attachment injury. If I know that my client has experienced a childhood attachment injury, I like to spend a great deal of time assessing the health of their social and intimate relationships. Whether the client is a teenager or an adult, the level of relational health is often very similar. With my teen clients, I have heard very incongruent statements such as "My friends make fun of me sometimes" or

"Although they have hurt me many times, I know they don't mean it in that way." I have also heard similar statements from adults such as "Yes, I know I am in an abusive relationship, but he/she loves me" or "As long as I keep the peace, our relationship is fine".

If I hear anything similar or remotely close, my counselor radar screams *trauma bond*.[1] This is when a mixture of fear and excitement is used to control and keep the victim trapped in the unhealthy relationship. It is a prime example of the cycle of abuse[2] in relation to abusive intimate relationships. It starts with a *lovey-dovey* phase, full of promises and gifts. Once that phase wears off, the anger and criticism begin, which then leads up to the direct attack (physical, emotional, or sexual). What keeps the victim going back to the offender is that he or she makes new promises again, buys gifts, and is truly the "nicest" person . . . until the tension builds again. This is what happens with domestic violence victims in particular. The bad truly does outweigh the good in most cases, but it is that 30 percent of the "good" that chains them and keeps them in bondage.

WHAT IS RELATIONAL HYPERVIGILANCE?

Hypervigilance consists of various triggers (activations) of the threat system such as loud noises (planes flying, doors slamming), closed doors, certain facial expressions, and pretty much anything that is a reminder of the earlier trauma (i.e., the razor for Mr. Grinch). An example would be a war veteran who is now back home and jumps on the floor every time he hears a plane fly over his house; or a woman who trembles at the sound of work boots walking on a hardwood floor because, as a child, that sound indicated that her dad was home. The sound produced so much fear because she was uncertain of whether he was in a good or bad mood. If he were in a bad mood, it most likely meant Mommy would get hit again.

For the sake of simplicity, we will only look at hypervigilance in the context of intimate relationships. As mentioned in the preface, I define relationally hypervigilant as a person who is supersensitive to real (or perceived) threats in an intimate relationship. This includes threats of rejection, abandonment, neglect, and abuse. A relationally hypervigilant individual will do all they can to prevent these threats from happening, even if it means clinging or running before they happen. They are often anxious about the other's behaviors, thoughts, and feelings, and they struggle with ambiguity because they "manage" life by being in control. This person often has to "steal" trust in order to trust (i.e., phone searching, social media snooping, requesting passwords, etc.).

Essentially, a relationally hypervigilant person is very low in trusting others and at times can have a negative view of self as well. This helps to produce an insecure attachment with both the self and others; particularly their intimate partner. The paradox is that this person can push safe people away and cling to unsafe people.

Common Factors Related To Hypervigilant Individuals

The Fears of Rejection, Abandonment, Neglect, and Abuse

An individual who has experienced a childhood attachment injury oftentimes has the fear of being rejected, abandoned, neglected, or continually abused and misused. Some of the more common client themes that I have encountered include the feeling of being used by others, a belief that they wouldn't be taken care of by anyone, and the constant thought that someone they cared about would soon leave them. These fears are very common and normal in this context.

At some point in your childhood, you may have felt that your parents or someone close to you rejected you. Maybe you had a B on your report card and they told you that you could've tried harder. Or maybe they questioned your every decision, causing you to feel that your own thoughts and feelings were wrong. You may have also felt that your mom or dad was never or rarely "there" in your life. Your mom could have been physically or emotionally unavailable because she was too busy worrying about her boyfriend … and all the ones that followed. These experiences, and other similar ones, planted the seeds related to the fears of rejection, abandonment, and neglect.

Fear of Losing Control

Another common fear is the fear of losing control. As a child you may have felt powerless, like you didn't have control over certain situations, so now, as an adult, you hold on to your sense of control with a death grip in order to feel safe. Having this intense urge to control produces considerable angst. We can become easily frustrated, irritated, and stressed out when things do not go as planned. When high levels of anxiety overcome us, our ability to rationalize clearly and make sound decisions is interrupted. It is almost as if our comfort blanket has been snatched away from us.

When we have this need to be in control, we also have a difficult time delegating tasks and asking for help. I struggled with this for quite some time. I never wanted to delegate tasks or ask for help because I figured it was just best if I did it myself. At least then I knew it would get done, and it would be done in the way I wanted it to. When I think about it now, it truly was a matter of low trust in others.

Another component of control is the fear that if you do not exert control, things will fall apart. I had a client once say that if she didn't allow her perfectionism to control her, she would not be successful. She went on to say that if she cut herself some slack and showed herself some compassion, she would not be good enough or worthy enough. Relinquishing the need to control is like letting go of how things have always been done, and that, in and of itself, can produce more fear.

 Fear of Being Controlled

Another part of the fear of losing control is the fear of being controlled. If you were controlled as a child and felt like you never had a voice, you may be the type that now resists anyone who you feel is trying to silence or suppress your voice. You may be very hypersensitive to others who are controlling and manipulative. This isn't necessarily a bad thing, but it can become a hindrance if nobody around you can provide you with criticism, feedback, correction, or direction without you becoming all defensive and feeling like they are trying to tell you what to do. So, essentially, what you end up with is a super control freak who doesn't like to be controlled.

Stolen Trust

Having low trust in others can cause us to have to "steal" it. Stolen trust is when we need to have proof of another's trustworthiness and loyalty prior to trusting him or her. You may feel the need to steal trust because you have never been able to fully trust anyone in your past; because of that, you never learned what it was to have pure trust. This may have developed from several experiences, including your parents saying they would do something or allow you to do something, but would rarely follow through on their word. This caused you to doubt people's sincerity when they gave you their *word* and *promise*.

So, for example, you may not trust that your spouse is faithful unless he or she gives you every password to every device and every account that needs a password. Or you may find yourself needing a minute-by-minute itinerary of their day, and if five minutes seem to be off, you begin to question their honesty. However, you may find that you are still not satisfied with this stolen trust, so you go the extra mile to try to catch them off guard to really be sure they aren't doing anything. You may think this way because you believe that if you ask them ahead of time, you give them time to think of a lie or delete any evidence. When it boils down to it, stolen trust is really just suspicion that is temporarily eased by bits and pieces of found evidence.

The Confusion of Being Loved and Injured by the Same Person

Childhood attachment injuries often begin in the household with a mother, father, or both. So what do you do when the person that is supposed to love and protect you is the same person that hurts and endangers you? As you can imagine, this produces great confusion in children because in one instance, they want to be comforted by their parents, and in the very next moment, they can fear for their life being in the arms of the same parent. This too is how trauma bonds are formed. Sadly enough, some children grow up thinking that love hurts; therefore, they find themselves in relationships with people who hurt them . . . because that's what love *is* to them.

HYPERVIGILANT TRAITS

Pros

Hypervigilant individuals often are pretty good non-verbal, body-language readers. They are very observant and are watching your every move. They have a highly alert protective system. They are watching the way you raise your eyebrows, the way you cross your legs, the way you fold your arms, the way your voice inflection changes, and even the way you clench your jaw. They can sense your fear, hurt, worry, anxiety, and even your rage. They are watching you like a hawk, trying to notice any sudden moves or changes that may indicate danger. Better yet, they are watching you like a dog. Dogs are also very perceptive. They are reading your facial expressions as well as changes in your mood, posture, gait, and even your physiology. So they essentially know what you are feeling, sometimes before you do. Just try it out: be sad around your dog, and then be happy around your dog. Notice how different its demeanor is toward you for both emotions. Just like dogs, hypervigilant people are focused on two things: "Is this a threat or is this a reward?"

Cons

Growing up in an inconsistent and unsafe environment (mentally, physically, or emotionally) requires you to be quick on your toes so that you can immediately move out of the line of fire. Hypervigilant individuals can often pick up on other's affect, even before a word is spoken, because they were trained in an environment where urgency and swift responses were the way to surviving. They learned what Mom or Dad's trigger points were, and they learned to read their body language very well so that they could predict what was going to happen next just by the look on their face or the tone in their voice. A downside to such swift judgments is that they may be too premature and end up with a false positive— especially if they are judging outside of the arena where the abuse took place.

For example, a woman may see the look of disappointment on her husband's face and run off crying, thinking he is going to abandon her. She makes this swift judgment because she generalizes her past onto her present and assumes that his look of disappointment means the same thing that her dad's look of disappointment meant when she was a teenager. Or maybe you have had someone repeatedly ask you, "What are you mad about?" While you repeat "nothing" over and over again, they refuse to believe you because your look of being in deep thought looks like an angry look they remember as a child.

WHO TENDS TO BE HYPERVIGILANT?

Hypervigilant individuals tend to have anxiety, and their most dominant attachment style is anxiously attached. It is important to know that avoidantly attached individuals may not display hypervigilance (see chapter 1 for the attachment discussion). Pure avoidantly attached individuals are not hypervigilant due, in part, to the low focus on threat-related cues. Anxiously attached people look for threats and analyze the situation to pieces while avoidantly attached individuals suppress, dismiss, or dissociate when faced with threats. So, basically, anxiously attached people see and keep gazing while avoidantly attached people see but ignore or divert their gaze (literally or internally).

If you feel that you are predominantly avoidantly attached but have hypervigilant tendencies, then recall that we can have a mixture of more than one attachment style. Even if avoidance dominates, just a hint of anxiety can spawn hypervigilance. That is the way I was. I was anxiously attached because I desired connection, but once I felt that I wasn't getting what I wanted or like I was going to be rejected, I just simply switched to an avoidantly attached style as my defense. That remained my primary style for quite some time. I did this because I wanted to be the "rejector" and not the rejected. I wanted to have control of whether you were in my life or not, not you.

MAIN TAKE AWAY POINT

The fears that you experienced in the past may still feel alive and real today. If you do not face those fears they will continue to rule your relationships today and tomorrow.

Free Training Video
Visit www.trillionsmall.com/book-mypast
for a free training on this chapter.

CHAPTER SIX

OVERCOMING RELATIONAL HYPERVIGILANCE: SELF-COMPASSION AS THE INFLECTION POINT

IN ORDER TO HAVE self-compassion, you have to have some sort of working knowledge of yourself. Unfortunately, one of the most difficult questions to answer is "Who are you?" We stumble with this question because we often spend very little time being introspective and reflective. When we are low in self-awareness, it is difficult to be high in self-compassion. This chapter will discuss ways to become an overall healthier you.

KNOW YOUR STORY

You can't have self-compassion for what you do not acknowledge or what you ignore. It is very difficult to read a closed book. Knowing your story begins with opening up your book of life and dusting off the pages of your past to bear witness and give a voice to all that has happened in your life. No, this does not mean you are dwelling in the past. It simply means taking the time to lift up the rug to remove all of the stuff you swept under there. The more you have swept under the rug, the more difficult and hazardous it is to walk over. Try putting a whole bunch of stuff under your living room rug and see if walking over it is easier or harder. It's harder, right? It is harder because stuff is not meant to live under rugs.

The reason why I enjoy doing EMDR with my clients (and personally) is because it allows us to give voice to what has happened. Once that has happened, it then allows us to tell the story in a new way. We are made up of many stories, but trauma often blocks many of our positive stories and makes our sad stories the ones that are most pervasive. Dealing with and healing from our past helps us to see the new stories we are creating every day. We no longer rearrange our lives based off what happened to us. Dealing with our past helps us to see it for what it was and then move on from it. Your past will always be a part of your story, but you must remember that is only volume 2 of your life. You have several other volumes that are great memories, and you still have many more volumes that need to be written.

The thing about childhood trauma is that the story was written *for* us. As adults we now have the pen and paper and can choose how the story will end. God has not called us to rewrite our story; that is impossible. But He has given us the ability to now finish the story. In a sermon,[1] Bishop Joseph Warren Walker III[2] stated that the author of a book always determines the end of a story, not the reader. Your family, friends, and foes are the readers of your story, but God is the author[3] of your story. How the story ends is not and has never been determined by others. God wants us to be co-laborers[4] (coauthors) with Him to make the end of our story the best ever.

Here are a few questions you can take the time to ponder on and answer in your journal to help you begin to give voice to your story:

- How have your experiences shaped you?
- How have they influenced you?
- What are your trigger points because of your experiences?
- What hurts your feelings?
- What makes you scared?
- What makes you worry?
- What do you over- or underreact to?
- What gets under your skin?
- What makes you furious?
- What makes you feel depressed?
- What makes you happy?

While answering these questions I want you to answer them as if you were that little child.

As adults we have the capability to rationalize, so when we look at our wounded child from an adult's perspective, we may think it is irrational. This is all in retrospect, obviously, so you may not recall exactly how you felt on the exact day and time, but you can draw a pretty good assumption based on how you respond today to similar stimuli. So, for example, you may not remember how you felt when your dad always yelled at you, but just think of how you feel today when someone yells at you! That should be a clue. Also, while "interacting" with our wounded self, it is a necessity to observe and interact from a heart filled with self-compassion.

KNOW YOUR BARRIERS AND DEFENSES

We discussed various carryover effects of childhood attachment injuries in chapter 2. Take some time now to look back over the list and refresh your memory of the ones you feel are your bricks. Although your defenses and coping are truly ways of self-protection, they can become your own barriers. What protected you as a child is now hurting you as an adult because what once was an adaptive way of coping is now maladaptive. It served you well, and maybe even saved your life, to dissociate as a child, but now, as an adult, it could be the barrier to learning how to cope in healthy ways. It served you well to run away when that person was trying to hurt you, but it is destroying your relationships when you run every time you have a disagreement with someone. Remember that the walls that we put up to give us a sense of strength are hindrances to our spiritual walk. God calls us to be humble, because in our weakness, He is strong.

I am aware that one of my defenses was to push people away and put myself in solitary confinement. Then, shortly after, I'd get mad that nobody was around, but I was the one that isolated myself in the first place!! Little by little, God began to reveal to me the various ways that I put up walls to protect myself. I found that many of my clients also had walls up, so I created a worksheet called "My Barriers & Defenses" (see appendix B) to help us learn what they were and how we could begin setting goals to remove them. This worksheet helps you to first identity all of the bricks that create your wall. The second column then helps you to identify why the brick was set in place to begin with. The question for this column is, "What is it (the brick) blocking or hiding?" A brick can be blocking both positive and negative things from coming to you. It may also be hiding something about yourself that you don't wish for others to see. Finally, the third column provides a place for you to brainstorm thoughts and ideas to help remove the brick.

My Barriers & Defenses Worksheet Example

The Brick	What is it Blocking (B) or Hiding (H)?	What do I need to remove it?
Compulsive Self-Reliance	B: Connection with others H: Fear of compassion	Secure attachment with self & others Self-Compassion

(Figure 3)

KNOW YOUR EMOTIONS

Are You Feeling?

The walls that we put up can be walls that separate us from others, or they can be walls that we put up within ourselves that separate the integration of our thoughts and emotions. The latter is also a form of compartmentalizing, avoiding, and numbing. When we put up a wall that block us from experiencing our emotions, we shortchange ourselves from living fully. When we make every effort to block the uncomfortable feelings and only want to feel the good feelings, we are missing out on viable moments of life. Life is full of mixed emotions, and when we limit ourselves to only a select few that make us feel good, we are living a limited life.

We must learn to be able to hold two seemingly contradicting emotions at the same time. When you begin to bring voice to your story, you may notice that you feel both sad and angry towards the offender. As more is cleaned from under your rug, you may then begin to feel joyful and liberated. But you may still feel angry, primarily at the fact that you didn't find freedom sooner.

What Are Your Emotions Saying?

In order to know our emotions, we must be comfortable listening to what they have to say. This means we cannot stuff them away when they make us uncomfortable. When I am teaching my clients the process of getting to know their emotions, the most frequent question is, "What do I do when they come?!" They have been so used to stuffing their emotions that when I ask them to actually *feel* their emotions, I see a hint of fear in their eyes. Knowing your emotions is simply building a relationship with yourself, just as you would with another person. When you want to know how a person feels about a particular thing you may ask, "How are you feeling?" or "What do you need right now?" or "Can I do anything to help you in this moment?" I encourage clients to ask themselves these questions (or ones that are similar) when emotions that make them uncomfortable bubble to the surface. In the beginning this will take much practice and intentionality because what I am asking them to do is to put a stopper in their long-lived cycle of stuffing their emotions.

Whose Emotion is This Anyway?

The final thing you need to be aware of when knowing your emotions is whether you are feeling your own emotions or someone else's. As an example, I have been around friends who make me feel depressed. Because I knew I wasn't depressed, this experience left me so confused that I began to ask the Lord about it. What He revealed to me was that I was experiencing *their* depression. Some of my clients have had similar situations with their family members. For example, if a client presents with a very specific fear or anxiety, more times than not that was the same fear or anxiety her parents had. So, because she grew up in that environment, what was theirs also became hers. The good news is that you may be carrying around somebody else's stuff! In order to know whose stuff it is, you may find it helpful to know your family history.

Let's Start Feeling

If you'd like to stop your long-lived cycle, then give what I tell my clients a try. When an uncomfortable emotion comes up, simply stop and ask yourself the following questions, and then follow these guidelines:

- What am I feeling?

- What just happened to cause me to feel this way?

- Is this my emotion or someone else's?
    - If it is someone else's, say: "This isn't my anxiety/fear/sadness/anger . . . and I choose not to carry it!" Then, hand it over to the Lord and leave it there.
    - If it is your emotion, ask yourself what your emotion is telling you that you may need in that moment (i.e., if you feel lonely, you may need to call a friend. Or, if you feel afraid, you may need to know that you are safe).

- Allow yourself to feel the emotion in the moment.
    - If you are feeling too overwhelmed, take several deep breaths until you feel calm enough to sit with your emotions.

- If you can, give yourself what you need (i.e., tell yourself that you are OK, that you can handle it, that you are a good enough person) and/or reach out to your support team to help cheer you along and encourage you when needed.

In this process of feeling, a good support team is vital. Fortunately, and unfortunately, we are at the mercy of others to get certain needs met. There are just some things that we need others to do for us. Hugging ourselves will only satisfy for so long. We are designed to be relational beings, so we all need the touch of others, whether we want to admit it or not. It is great to begin building your support team with a counselor, but you are limited to a mere fifty minutes per week with them; you will need more than that on your team.

KNOW YOUR FEARS

One of the reasons we block our emotions is because of a fear; the fear of losing control and being overtaken by a sea of emotions is one. It almost feels like you have been shaken up like a soda: you know that if you immediately take off the cap, you will flow all over the place and it will be a horrible mess. This fear is understandable, especially when the control of your emotions was the only thing you had control over as a child. You couldn't really control what you did or what was done to you, but you could control, to a certain degree, what you thought and what you felt. You may not have been able to win the verbal fight literally, but you could win in your mind by choosing to have an intense internal hatred for that person. As we have been learning, though, what we do internally can have adverse effects on our life.

Other fears you may have are fears of failure, rejection, abandonment, and of not being perfect or accepted. These fears are all socially and relationally crippling! They do not enable us to be ourselves, and they do not enable others to be who they are. If you are too worried about not being rejected and abandoned, the person that you are with is likely worried about the eggshells they have to walk on to ensure that they work overtime to make you feel loved, cherished, and good enough. If you instead choose to face and deal with your fears, your relationships should begin to look a lot healthier. You will no longer try to be something that you are not, so you will no longer be consumed by debilitating fears. You will begin to have more times of peace and calmness in your life instead of constant internal and external chaos and turmoil that may be driven, in part, by your hypervigilance.

KNOW YOUR NEEDS

Knowing what our needs are is a pivotal moment in our cycle of relational hypervigilance. If we do not know what our needs are, it will be very difficult to get them met. It's like asking a husband to read his wife's mind; it isn't happening unless she tells him (with the exception of times of attunement and discernment). Even the all- knowing God tells us to make our requests know to Him (Phil. 4:6), so there is something to the act of actually verbalizing what we want, desire, and are in need of. It may be cliché, but it is true: a closed mouth never got fed.

Our needs are often tied to the wound. The fulfillment of our need is the antidote to where it hurts. When we are hypervigilant, we often *need* to know that we are not rejected, that we are not being ignored, that we are cared about, and that we are good enough. Most importantly, we need to know that we are seen and heard, and that our connection with another is safe, secure, and solid.

Another common need that we all have is to know and be known by others. Getting this need met first requires us becoming comfortable in a place of vulnerability and transparency. If you are going to allow yourself to be known by others that you trust, you will have to become comfortable being *naked and unashamed*,[5] metaphorically speaking. Knowing and being known is a process of reciprocation. The flow is interrupted when only one person is open and authentic. It takes two to tango in this dance of knowing.

If you are afraid of letting others know you due to the fear that they will reject you if they really knew "who you were," then try starting with letting Jesus get to know you. Yes, He knows all things, but just like Adam and Eve, our sin and our wounds cause us to hide from Him. Little by little, allow your wounds to be exposed to God, who desires to know you in the most intimate way! That's something to shout hallelujah about! Even at our lowest and "bleeding" times, He desires to know us. Just like the woman with the issue of blood,[6] God wanted to KNOW who touched the hem of His garment. It didn't matter that she came to Him bloody and all; she was that important to Him.

Becoming aware of and accepting the fact that we have needs can be quite scary, especially for those who have tried for so long to present as strong and needy-less. The truth of the matter is that we all are "needy" to a certain degree, and that is not a bad thing. We were never designed to live in a silo. If the woman with the issue of blood did not humble herself and muster up the courage and faith to touch Jesus, she probably would have died on the outskirts of the city, alone. But she refused to, so she admitted that she had a need that nobody else could fulfill and she pressed her way in to make her need known to the master healer, Jesus Christ.

❤

Are you willing to die alone, both literally and figuratively, because you are too prideful to admit that you have needs? Are you willing to continue to miss out on healthy relationships because you are too stubborn or ashamed to admit that you have a wound? Will you allow embarrassment and fear to continue to rob you of the joys of life? If you answered no to these questions, then taking the time to know your story, barriers, defenses, emotions, fears, and needs is a route you can take to overcome the challenges and obstacles that hypervigilance may have caused in your relationships.

Most of the necessary work to overcome relational hypervigilance will have to be done in you. What is produced OUTSIDE of you will begin to be a healthy reflection of the work that is taking place WITHIN you. Everything we need we already have within, the greatest element being the Holy Spirit! If you have not received the gift of the Holy Spirit by way of salvation, then I'd like to pray a prayer of salvation with you. If you'd like, pray this simple prayer and receive Jesus Christ as your Lord and Savior today:

God, I desire a relationship with You. I ask that You forgive me of all of my sins, the ones that I am aware of and the ones that I am not aware of. I accept You into my life and ask that You cleanse me from the inside out. I believe in my heart and I confess with my mouth that Your son, Jesus, is Lord and that He died for my sins and rose on the third day. Come into my heart and be Lord over my life today. In Jesus' name, Amen.

If you prayed that prayer for the first time, welcome to the family! You are now saved! The Holy Spirit will begin to work in your life to mature you as His child. I encourage you to find a solid Bible-based church (if you don't have one already) and connect with like-minded Christians who are walking the same faith journey as you are now. The past is behind you and the best is ahead of you. Walk boldly in your new relationship with God, Jesus Christ, and the Holy Spirit. Now, everything you need truly is IN you!

MAIN TAKE AWAY POINT

We are hurt and hindered by what we don't know. Get knowledge and live.

Free Training Video
Visit www.trillionsmall.com/book-overcoming
for a free training on this chapter.

CHAPTER SEVEN

THE OTHER SIDE OF RELATIONAL HYPERVIGILANCE IS RELATIONAL DISCERNMENT

ONE DAY, AS I was in prayer, God revealed that our external relationships are correlated with our internal relationship with self. When the self is healthy, we attract and are drawn to healthy. When the self is unhealthy, we attract and are drawn to unhealthy (recall the trauma bond discussion in chapter 5). I have seen this magnetic force work in my personal life.

In one of my counseling sessions, my counselor and I were talking about my relationships. As I was talking, he obviously was seeing patterns that I was completely oblivious to. He stopped and looked at me and said, "Trillion, it seems like you are attracted to dismissive men." When he first said this, I was thinking *Umm, no, I am not . . . that would be stupid . . . why would I be attracted to men that don't pay much attention to me*?! Since he made that statement near the end of the session, I had an entire week before the next time I saw him to really ponder his statement. When I left I began to evaluate all of my relationships that I had had, even the ones that I desired, but didn't have. Sure enough, every man was dismissive in some form or fashion! As I processed it some more, I came to the conclusion that I was attracted to men like my biological father. I was attracted to dismissive, unresponsive, and selfish men. That is what shaped my first experience with men, so that is what I was drawn to.

I thank God for BUTS, though! I should've gone down a horrible path . . . BUT God! I also praise Him for self-awareness and revelation! After that session, I made it my goal to break that cycle for good! It took (and still does take) intentionality on my end to refuse to chase after or crave the attention of a man who doesn't have my best interest in mind! The moment I made this shift in my life, I began attracting men (and people in general) in my life who cared to know me and were not in it for their own selfish ambitions! Once I changed internally, I was able to change what came to me externally!

HOW TO MAKE THE TRANSITION?

One of the tasks of shifting from relational hypervigilance to relational discernment is to modify your defenses to fit your setting. If you are hypervigilant, you already have defenses in place that are likely deeply rooted from childhood. What we want to do is shift those maladaptive defenses and adjust them (or remove them) so that our interactions with others are healthy. The goal is to live a long healthy life, and in order to do that, we need healthy relationships. So here is the key:

You need A.A.I.R. to B.R.E.A.T.H.E. to L.I.V.E.

The following are things you will need to shift from relational hypervigilance to relational discernment:

A. **Awareness of yourself.** You have lived with yourself your entire life, but do you really know you? When the layers are pulled back, what is at your core? What has God wired in your genetic and spiritual DNA to make you uniquely you?

A. **Acceptance of yourself.** There is only one you, so revel in the fact that God thought enough of you to never duplicate you (even if you are a twin, you are not 100 percent alike). If God made you that way, then He calls it good. From the way you look to the way you walk to the way you interact with others—even down to the way your heart beats. Embrace all of you.

I. **Inclusion of all parts of you**. There may be parts of you that you wish to get rid of, such as the part of you that really feels emotions or even the child part of you that endured a lot. We must become comfortable with all of us, not just parts of us. It is important that we do not become fragmented by compartmentalizing or splitting ourselves off.

R. **Revelation of who you are.** You will begin to experience freedom when you really begin to see yourself the way God sees you. The astounding revelations that you are fearfully and wonderfully made, that He loved you even before He created you, and that He loves you even as an imperfect person really begin to pluck at your heart- strings if you let Him in.[1] Scripture no longer will sound cliché, but will become truth to you as you view your life from His eyes.

To

B. **Be.** Once you begin to realize who you are, you will no longer have the urge to *do* for the sake of acceptance and recognition. In *being* is where you realize that, no matter what you do or don't do, you will always be worthy. It isn't about what you do . . . it's about who you be (are).

R. **Rest.** When we learn to just *be*, resting comes a little bit more naturally. You are no longer the hamster on the wheel, spinning to no avail. When you were running from your emotions, you could never rest. Now that you have learned to just be, you can now find rest in stillness and solitude rather than fear and anxiety.

E. **Exhale.** As you begin to slow your running pace, you will be able to breathe much more easily. By going at a more slow and steady pace, you are able to unpack all of your baggage. If we inhale but never exhale, we will eventually find ourselves passed out somewhere. Let it all go.

A. **Allow your wounds to be exposed.** When you allow yourself to become more open and less defensive, your wounds will be exposed. This is a good thing. We want to give the wound the air and space that it needs. When you first take the bandage off, you may feel ashamed of the scar or the sight of blood, but it is OK . . . Jesus doesn't have a weak stomach. He can handle your wound.

T. **Talk about your story.** As you air your wounds out give voice to each scar. Tell the story of how you received each unique wound.

H. **Heal in this process.** God once told me that we heal in community. So as you are telling your story, you are healing in the process.

E. **Expect it to take some time**. You do not have to rush this phase of your life. It may take some time to sift through all of your past hurts and to dig up some deep roots. Give yourself more than just a week to heal!

To

L. **Let love in.** If you started off afraid of compassion, then you may find this a challenge. But the only way the wound will heal is if you stitch it up and put ointment on it . . . and in this case, your stitch and ointment is love. If you do not have trusting friends or family members who can love on you, then pray that God will send you friends who will. Remember, most importantly, that His love is what heals us all.

I. **Include others in your process.** Remember it is OK to ask for help and for your needs to be met. One of the most freeing gifts I was ever given was the gift to be able to tell someone, "No, I am not OK." I give you that gift today as well! We all need somebody to walk with us on our journey. Even Jesus said it wasn't good for man to be alone.[2]

V. **Shift from victim to victor.** When you used to tell your story, it was a sad blues song. But now, when you retell your story, you can tell it from a place of strength, courage, and hope! You can't say that you are free and still walk around with the chains around your neck. No longer are you the victim or the prisoner, you are a redeemed and set-free victor!

E. **Embrace your new way of interacting.** Welcome to a new way of living. The past is no longer present, so let's create our future by being present in the moment. The new you really does look good on you! Say goodbye to toxic relationships and say hello to life-giving relationships.

WHAT IS DISCERNMENT?

Now that you are resting in your new normal, your relational hypervigilance, with some adjustments, can be used as relational discernment. As mentioned in the preface, I define relational discernment as having the ability to perceive people in an accurate manner without having foreknowledge of them. You can discern both positive and negative things. Discernment is a viable tool in making wise decisions about whom you choose to connect with—and disconnect with—in relationships. The way I have experienced it is by having a sense of *knowing.* Sometimes you can't explain how or why, but you just know.

Make Use of Your Senses
In Hebrews 5:11-14, Paul expresses the importance of maturing your senses to understand and to discern between good and evil:

I have a lot more to say about this, but it may be hard for you to follow since you've become dull in your understanding. By this time, you ought to be teachers yourselves, yet I feel like you want me to reteach you the most basic things that God wants you to know. It's almost like you're a baby again, coddled at your mother's breast, nursing, not ready for solid food. No one who lives on milk alone can know the ins and outs of what it means to be righteous and pursue justice; that's because he is only a baby. But solid food is for those who have come of age, for those who have learned through practice to distinguish good from evil. (The Voice)

Essentially, what Paul appears to be saying is that it takes developed spiritual senses to learn to discern. The way to develop your senses is to use them in practice. We don't expect a one-year-old to know to look both ways to cross the road, but we do expect an eighteen-year-old to because they have gotten plenty of practice crossing many streets, both with someone else and by themselves.

As Paul has said, some of us are like one-year-old babies, still drinking milk, and not aware that there could be danger if we do not look both ways before crossing. On the other hand, there are some of us who have matured and have mastered the ability to cross the street safely. How? The experiences that train us to distinguish when it is safe to cross and when it is not are those times when we are able to practice with others, or they may be times of trial and error, after being screamed at, for example, for playing in the street.

Continuing with this metaphor, the one-year-old child is representative of the relationally hypervigilant person; even if they have a sense for danger, they still run into it carelessly and, once in it, become frantic about how to stay safe. Once they are in the street, they begin spinning in circles trying to avoid danger, never realizing that all they had to do was get out of the street to remove themselves from danger. Then you have the eighteen-year-old, who is representative of the relationally discerning person: much more mature and watchful for danger. They look for danger, and if the coast is clear, they are confident walking in the street; however, if they sense danger, they know how to quickly maneuver out of the way to a place of safety.

This type of discernment takes practice, though. It takes utilizing and stretching all ten of our senses. We are familiar with our five natural senses (hearing, seeing, smelling, tasting, and feeling); the other five senses are the same, but they're used in the spirit realm instead. Spiritual senses come into play when someone says, "I can spot or smell a rat a mile away" (in reference to a negative person) . . . or when you are around someone new and start getting that eerie feeling about them like something just doesn't seem right, and you later find out that they really are "crazy" . . . or when a domestic violence victim says that she knew her husband wasn't right well before he even put his hands on her.

Individuals who have eyes and ears and limbs but are unable to use them have an internal problem, not an external problem; the same is true of your spiritual senses. If your spiritual senses are not working, take time to do an internal check-up. You may have an internal nerve disconnected or a spiritual infection that is affecting your ability to see, hear, or feel God. Maybe there is sin in your life that is blocking the reception.[3] If so, repent and receive a clean slate so that you can have untainted vision, hearing, and touch reception from the Holy Spirit.

What Is the Difference Between Relational Hypervigilance and Relational Discernment?

Relational discernment isn't based solely on how you feel. Relational hypervigilance is when you are driven by your emotions. It can even be used as a manipulative or controlling strategy in a relationship. Relational discernment is when you listen to wisdom, even if your emotions are screaming something different. Discernment is being wise and vigilant, not hypervigilant. It doesn't seek to control or manipulate, but seeks knowledge in order to bring about a sense of balance and peace in relationships. Relational discernment looks internally at a man's heart to determine his character, but relational hypervigilance looks at the outward appearance and behaviors.

You can look straight into a person's eyes and discern their character. You can look and discern if their motives with you are pure. The eyes are the windows to the soul where the heart resides. Luke

11:33-36 states, "No one, when he has lit a lamp, puts it in a secret place or under a basket, but on a lampstand, that those who come in may see the light. The lamp of the body is the eye. Therefore, when your eye is good, your whole body also is full of light. But when your eye is bad, your body also is full of darkness. Therefore take heed that the light which is in you is not darkness. If then your whole body is full of light, having no part dark, the whole body will be full of light, as when the bright shining of a lamp gives you light."

The eyes tell all. Look in a person's eyes and discern for the light or darkness in their soul. We see God teaching Samuel to use this strategy of looking into the heart when He had him anoint the next king. God told him not to look at the outward appearance of the men he was evaluating, but to look deeper into the man's heart [through his eyes] (1 Sam. 16:7).

HOW TO TRAIN YOUR SENSES

First Things First

Watch and be sober. First Peter 5:8 says, "Be sober, be vigilant; because your adversary the devil walks about like a roaring lion, seeking whom he may devour." If we are not sober, we can easily mistake a wolf in sheep's clothing[4] to be an authentic sheep. Remember, it is not about what people look like on the outside; it's all about what they look like underneath the façade. Being drunk distorts your judgment, hindering you from distinguishing between what is real and what is just an illusion, what is holy and what is unholy, and what is clean and what is unclean.[5] Finally, you can't see what you don't look for. Open your eyes and be watchful.

Use peace as an indicator. In my first book,[6] I talk about how our level of peace is an indicator as to whether we are in the right place or not. Our level of peace can be an indicator to help us to discern those around us. A chaotic, disordered mind cannot be at peace. If we are completely in peace, that is our green light. If we are 50/50, we need to slow down and take more time to discern. If we are not at peace at all, we need to use that red flashing light as a warning to take the nearest exit! According to Philippians 4:7, the peace of God guards our heart and our minds. God's peace is protection for us. If you are not at peace, then don't be a fool led by emotions and keep moving forward in a relationship.

Have a stable mind. Isaiah 26:3 reminds us that God will keep those in perfect peace whose minds are stayed on Him. This means that a wavering mind is not a mind at rest and, therefore, is not a mind at peace. According to Proverbs 4:23-27 (MSG), we are to keep vigilant watch over our hearts and keep our eyes straight ahead so that we do not waiver due to distractions. James 1:8 even calls wavering people "double-minded." We cannot waver in our sea of emotions. Either we will believe in this or we will believe in that. We cannot fluctuate. When seeking wisdom to help you discern, you must believe and not doubt. Be stable in your decision-making.

RVT: Relational Vigilance Training (aka Relational Discernment)

The YMCA has Vigilance Awareness Trainings (VAT) where they teach their lifeguards how to be on the alert for what is out of place in their zone (i.e., someone flailing their arms while their head is coming above and below water). RVT is the exact same thing: developing not just the natural senses but also the spiritual senses to pick up on people in our "zone" who are out of place. Below you will find a list of items to help you in this process. Although this list is numbered, it is not a matter of sequence of events, so one is not necessarily a prerequisite for the next.

1. Know what your "go to" attachment style is.

Anxiously attached individuals need to turn the vigilance down, and avoidantly attached individuals need to turn it up. I say this because anxious people often read too much into things while avoidant people don't see enough. This is due, in part, to them making themselves not see (by dissociating, as we talked about in chapter 2).

2. Develop a secure base with someone you feel safe in expressing yourself openly with.

Having the space to do so allows you the room to practice knowing and understanding what you are feeling and experiencing with someone else. This space helps you to trust your own thoughts and feelings.

3. Get out of your feelings.

Yes, I want you to trust your thoughts and feelings so that you do not doubt when God speaks to you, but you cannot make a discerning and wise decision based on how you feel. Your feelings can be deceiving, so you must learn to regulate your own emotions.

4. Move from quick judgment to well-thought-out and deliberate judgment.

If you are hypervigilant, you are probably used to being very swift and impulsive in your decision-making. Take the time to slow down to assure you are making a wise decision. Stop and look both ways before you cross the street. Your first instinct often will be right, but it can also be flawed at times, especially if it is polluted with emotions. If it is, simply take the time to clean your filters out.

5. See things for what they are.

I do believe that there is good in all of us, but at times we use our optimism to overrule the warning signs we are receiving about a person. If the lights are flashing red, your hopes of how great they could be do not matter. It is tempting to see the good in the midst of the bad, but see the evil for what it is: evil. Hindsight is always 20/20, but let's work on getting our foresight 20/20 as well.

6. Develop a tolerance for uncomfortable feelings.

Sometimes what you are given as you discern will be uncomfortable and what you do not want to know.

This is understandable, but you must develop a tolerance for uncomfortable feelings so that you do not ignore what is right and uncomfortable.

7. Be prepared to deal with rejection.

This one may have caused your heart to jump. You mean to tell me that I am spending time to overcome the fear of rejection to get back to a place of rejection? Yes; oh the paradox of God's plans sometimes. When you begin to discern in your relationships, God may show you things He would have you share with others, and He may even show you things that require you to make changes that others won't like. I won't spend time talking about the prophetic, but I have found that those who are prophetic have a high anointing for discernment. However, you will be dealing with this rejection from a place of healing and health, not with anxiety and fear (like you used to).

8. You can't watch everyone and everything, so you have to watch for a break in the flow of the spirit.

Be sure that when you are watching, you are watching with a new set of lenses, not with the same old lenses of your past. What was a threat to you then most likely isn't a threat to you now. When you notice a break in the flow, test the spirit by the Spirit within you. What you think is a break may not be one; conversely, what you do not see as a break may well be. Read Acts 16:17-18 and Luke 7:36-50 to see examples. Paul cast out a demon in a woman who seemingly was saying all the right things about God, but she was a break in the flow. On the other hand, Simon frowned at the sinful woman who poured perfume on Jesus' feet because he thought she was a break in the flow, but she really wasn't.

9. Be still and know that He is God.

When you are rested and grounded in the Lord, you are able to make sound decisions. Be still and know that God will help you to see what you need to see when you need to see it.

WHAT MAKES YOU DIFFERENT?

You may have wondered why others went through the exact same thing as you but ended up having a nervous breakdown or being hospitalized, or worse, committing suicide. What sets you apart is what you have on the inside of you. No matter how despondent and broken you feel, if you have but a speck of light from the Holy Spirit in you, it makes a world of difference. That speck of light gives you hope, keeps you in your right mind, helps you find your way back home even if you wander away, and makes you like elastic rubber so even if you fall down, you always bounce back!

PRAYER OF ACTIVATION

Activating your relational discernment is just like having a dimmer switch. If you want to increase your ability, then turn the knob up to increase the light you are exposed to. If you desire to increase in discernment, then pray this activation prayer:

Dear Lord, thank You for binding up my broken heart, and thank You for setting me free from the chains of my past. I desire to use my experiences for the good to help deliver people out of similar situations such as myself. I also desire change in my life. I have broken the cycle of childhood abuse and I declare and decree that I will set the stage for the next generations to follow. Help me to do this by disconnecting from those who harm me and by connecting with those who are in line with Your will for my life. I ask for more wisdom and discernment now, Lord. Begin to train my spiritual senses to be able to test spirits to know whether they are from You or from the enemy. Give me opportunities to learn how to hear Your voice. I pray for Your strength and guidance as I go through this process. I plead the blood of Jesus over my life, and I pray a hedge of protection all around me so that no weapon formed against me shall prosper. Give me the grace, favor, and mercy to endure, even if the transition from hypervigilance to discernment is uncomfortable. Give me the will and grace to stick with it. Thank You in advance for all these things. In Jesus name, Amen.

AFTER YOU HAVE BEEN HEALED, TURN BACK AND HELP SOMEONE ELSE

Soon, very soon, you will be given opportunities to break the cycle in your family. You may not get it the first, second, or even third time, but do not give up. You will succeed if you endure to the end! I encourage you to stick with the process and deal with your internal wounds and defenses because they can hinder your relationship with God and delay you from having the relationships that you truly desire. God won't put new wine into old wine skin. If your past is still present, your future cannot come.

If you take nothing else away from this book, I hope that you at least will hear me when I say that your past had a purpose, and it can be used as a key for unlocking the answers to what on earth you are here for. Your history is a roadmap to your destiny. Don't let what you have gone through be wasted. After you receive healing, turn back . . . and help someone just like you.

There is hope for the wounded and caged child, and that hope starts with the work in you! Go, be free, and help free others! That, my friends, is your mission. I hope that you will accept it.

MAIN TAKE AWAY POINT

God can take what was meant to hurt us and use it to bless us. He gives us beauty when life hands us ashes.

Free Training Video
Visit www.trillionsmall.com/book-relationaldiscernment for a free training on this chapter.

CHAPTER NOTES

CHAPTER 1

1. According to the International Society for the Study of Trauma and Dissociation, dissociation is a word that is used to describe the disconnection or lack of connection between things usually associated with each other. Learn more at www.isst-d.org.

2. Eye Movement Desensitization Reprocessing (EMDR) is a psychotherapy treatment used to help alleviate the distress caused by past trauma experiences. Learn more at http://www.emdr.com/faqs.html.

3. Post-Traumatic Stress Disorder (PTSD) is a psychiatric disorder that can occur following a traumatic incident.

4. Developmental trauma is a psychiatric disorder related to childhood trauma, first identified by Bessel van der Kolk, MD. (It has not been confirmed as an official disorder by the Diagnostic and Statistical Manual of Mental Disorders [DSM], however.)

5. Internal Family Systems (IFS) is a therapy modality. Learn more at http://www.selfleadership.org/outline-of-the-Internal-family-systems-model.html.

6. John Bowlby was the leading attachment theorist.

7. K. Bartholomew and L. M. Horowitz, "Attachment styles among young adults: A test of a four-category model," *Journal of Personality and Social*

Psychology 61 (1991): 226-44.

8. "What's Your Romantic Attachment Style?" *About. com,* http://psychology.about.com/library/quiz/ bl-attachment-quiz.htm.

CHAPTER 2

1. B. Soenens, M. Vansteenkiste, P. Luyten, B. Duriez, and L. Goossens, "Maladaptive perfectionistic self-representations: The mediational link between psychological control and adjustment," *Personality and Individual Differences* 38 (2005): 487-98.

2. *The New Strong's Concise Concordance and Vine's Concise Dictionary of the Bible* (Nashville, TN: Thomas Nelson, 1999), s.v. "teleios."

3. Iron Man is a character from the movie *Iron Man* who put on his full body armor when it was time to fight.

CHAPTER 4

1. K. D. Neff, "The development and validation of a scale to measure self- compassion," *Self and Identity* 2 (2003): 223-50.

2. Paul Gilbert, "Compassion and cruelty: A biopsychosocial approach." In *Compassion: Conceptualisations, Research and Use in Psychotherapy,* ed. Paul Gilbert (London: Routledge, 2005), n.p.

3. Rom. 8:28.

4. 1 Pet. 5:10.

CHAPTER 5

1. *The Betrayal Bond: Breaking Free of Exploitive*

Relationships (Deerfield Beach, FL: Health Communications, Inc., 1997), a book by Patrick Carnes, is a great resource that goes more in depth about trauma bonding and how to break free from it.

2. Lenore E. Walker developed the cycle of abuse in 1979 to explain the behavior patterns in abusive relationships.

CHAPTER 6

1. This sermon, given on July 19, 2015, is titled "After All of This, It's Got to Happen" in the series titled *Defining Moments.*

2. Bishop Joseph Warren Walker III is the senior pastor of Mount Zion Baptist Church in Nashville, Tennessee. He is also the Presiding Bishop of the Full Gospel Fellowship.

3. Heb. 12:2.

4. 1 Cor. 3:9.

5. Gen. 2:25.

6. Luke 8:43-48.

CHAPTER 7

1. Ps. 139:14; Jer. 1:5; Rom. 5:8.

2. Gen. 2:18.

3. Isa. 59:1-2; Jer. 5:25.

4. Matt. 7:15.

5. Lev 10:10.

6. In my book *Internal Navigator* (Bloomington, IN: WestBow Press, 2013), I discuss how the Holy Spirit is our internal GPS and how we need Him to help guide us in all decision-making, so blocking that reception would not be beneficial for us.

APPENDIX A

A few years, ago I stumbled upon a book that I wrote in the third grade. When I found it, I was actually in search of little Trillion. Although grown, I felt there was a big piece of my life missing, one that I knew nothing about. I believe that I dissociated at times; there were other times where my brain just never encoded (stored) the memories because they were too overwhelming. I'm not a children's therapist, but I have some working knowledge of play and art therapy, so I read and re-read my book, analyzing my pictures for clues as to what I was experiencing as a child. It became very apparent that I was a fearfully anxious child with avoidance tendencies.

I am publishing my third-grade book as an outward expression of giving voice and recognition to my little self. For so long, she didn't have a voice, but now she has a published book. Giving her a voice started with the work in me, however. So I give you this challenge today: become intentional about exploring the little you inside and have self-compassion as you learn his or her story. Once you do, give it voice, because your story matters! Your voice is your story. Your story is your testimony. Your testimony is your purpose! Go, walk in your purpose today. Be free and help free others from the same bondage, as Luke 22:31-32 instructs us. You will be sifted as wheat, but take heart because you are promised that your faith will not fail. Once you have overcome, reach back and strengthen your brothers and sisters in Christ.

The book in your hands is my way of reaching back. How will *you* reach back?

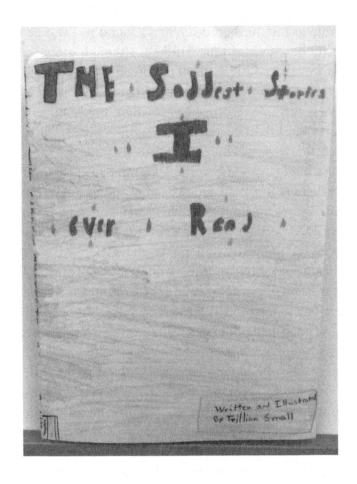

Once there was a book called Keep
our library books clean. One day a boy
went to the library and got two books to read.
That little boy had loved to read and
write. A few days later he wrote a story
called You can Learn by Reading Good
Books. He only got to a paragraph because
he had to go to bed and that paragraph
said, I am so smart because I read lots
of good books from the library. The next
morning that little boy wanted to go to the library
but he had to go to his cousins house at
eight o'clock A.M. But his mom said you can
read all you want because yesterday your
cousin won the lottery. He said every time
you can read all you want to read. The
little boy said I count the kind of book I want
his mother that just what your cousin said. When
they got there the boys mom started to say
something. She said my boy want to read your
books y'all got. The boys cousin said that's

fine with me if that's what he likes to do.
The boy went to the big shelfs with long
some short shelves. He picked up about that had
thick pages no pictures but he didn't care. He
read a paragraph he said, that a paragraph. I read was nice.
He read the rest of the page and another item

then he sat down and made hisself
comfortable and read half of the book.
he said he had a few more pages left.
He asked if he can take the book home
his cousin said it was ok but bring it back

In at least one week. On Monday he was all
almost done with the book, he had seven
more chapters till the end of the book

2

It was a good begining. When he
got down to the fourth to the last chapter
it was sad because a little girls
father died in a war. She was only five
years old. Luckly she had a mother that
could take care of her, but that girl was
so scared to go to daycare because of what happend
to her dear father. Every time she
goes to daycare she says to her
mother, mom I love you and
while I'm gone please don't get hurt
and dieI will always love you. Bye Bye
momlove you.

1

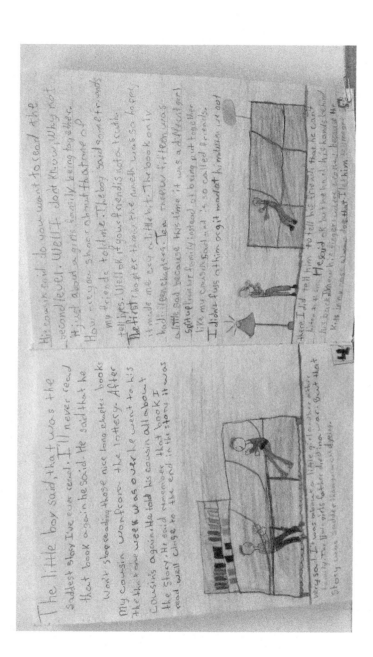

The little boy said, that was the saddest story I've ever read. I'll never read that book again, he said. He said that he won't stop reading those nice long chapter book.

My cousin won from the lottery. After that one week was over, he went to his cousins again. He told his cousin all about the story. He said remember that book I read will cling to the end. In the story it was

peg so I. It was always a time go to other other. peg so I. Two girls father had no car. But that story was sadder than on paper.

His cousin told, do you want to read the second level. Well I don't know, why not. He just about a girls family being together. How are you shoes about that one of my friends told me. The boy said some friends my friends. Well ok if your friend is nice to each other lives.

The first chapter that the ninth week was so happy, made me cry a little. Hehe. The book only half way chapters. Ten new fifteen chapters. A little bad because this time it was a different girl. Split up their family instead of being put together like my cousin said and it's so called friends.

I didn't fuss at him or get mad at him, even it not

Here I did tell him to tell his friends that he cant hem x x x. He said R but the his back. I know he had tiger... because he this one was slow, sad that I kick him slimer it not

of his other lies about the third book. I was amazed about what he told me because it was true. When I returned it I asked him have you stopped fighting your friends and those books I read. Remember what you told me about your friends telling you all about the books but they where lies. I'm sorry and I hope you now do pain. Me my apology. well I will if you stop putting your hands behind your back.

and his crossing your fingers. I will not cross my fingers. Now will you ask me yes or yes.

If you want to read these books just ask your cousin. The third book I got to the ninth chapter I read made me stay up all night because the book was about a man that comes in your basement and make all this smoke noise. Those sounds realy give me the creeps I wanted to throw the book away.

My name is Trilla Sma.11 My favorite hobby is basketball. In my spare time I like to play with my friends and take walks around my apartment. I go to Cahola Heights Elementary School. I am in the third grade. I love to read and write.

Summary
This book is about a boy and his cousin. The cousin won a lottery. Now He has a shelf full of books. Read this book and you'll find out more.

APPENDIX B

My Barriers & Defenses

The Brick	What is it blocking or hiding?	What do I need to remove it?

Get powered up, get into position, and get all that God has for you. Finding our way through life can be difficult, but aren't you so excited that God gave us such a valuable gift upon salvation? Going through life no longer has to be a path of uncertainty.

Residing in you is your very own personal Navigational System that is ready to take you to new places and to new heights in your life. If you have questions about your purpose, how to obtain your promises, or what you should be doing in this season of your life, then this is a resource for you.

Are you ready to allow the Holy Spirit to take total control of the steering wheel of your life and guide you to your destiny? Crack open this book, hop right in, and let's get ready for the ride!

Begin to live on purpose for purpose today!

STAY CONNECTED

@TrillionSmall

https://www.linkedin.com/in/trillionsmall

www.youtube.com/trillionsmall

Website: www.trillionsmall.com

CPSIA information can be obtained at www.ICGtesting.com
Printed in the USA
LVOW04s0503151015

458353LV00001B/1/P